International Perspectives on Education Reform
Gita Steiner-Khamsi, Editor

International Aid to Education

Power Dynamics in an Era of Partnership

Francine Menashy

Foreword by Steven J. Klees

TEACHERS COLLEGE PRESS

TEACHERS COLLEGE | COLUMBIA UNIVERSITY

NEW YORK AND LONDON

Published by Teachers College Press, 1234 Amsterdam Avenue, New York, NY 10027

Copyright © 2019 by Teachers College, Columbia University

Design by Jeremy Fink.

Chapter 3 contains a figure from "Unequal partners? Networks, Centrality, and Aid to International Education," by F. Menashy and R. Shields, 2017, *Comparative Education*, 53(4), p. 495–517. Reprinted with permission of Taylor & Francis Ltd, http://www.tandfonline.com.

Chapter 3 contains text from "Unequal partners? Networks, Centrality, and Aid to International Education," by F. Menashy and R. Shields, 2017, *Comparative Education*, 53(4), p. 495–517. Reprinted with permission of Taylor & Francis Ltd, http://www.tandfonline.com.

Chapter 4 contains text from "Understanding the Roles of Non-State Actors in Global Governance: Evidence from the Global Partnership for Education," by F. Menashy, 2016, *Journal of Education Policy*, 31(1), p. 98–118. Reprinted with permission of Taylor & Francis Ltd, http://www.tandfonline.com.

Chapter 4 contains text from "Multi-stakeholder Aid to Education: Power in the Context of Partnership," by F. Menashy, 2018, *Globalisation, Societies and Education*, 16(1), p. 13–26. Reprinted with permission of Taylor & Francis Ltd, http://www.tandfonline.com

Library of Congress Cataloging-in-Publication Data is available at loc.gov

ISBN 978-0-8077-6128-1 (paper)
ISBN 978-0-8077-6181-6 (hardcover)
ISBN 978-0-8077-7768-8 (ebook)

Printed on acid-free paper
Manufactured in the United States of America

Contents

Foreword

Two decades ago, the theme of the Oxford International Conference on Education and International Development was "Poverty, Power, and Partnership." At the time, I wrote a blog post whose title rearranged these words into "The Poverty of Partnership Without Power," which captured for me the problematic nature of discussions of partnership—then and now. Unfortunately, in the ensuing years, the use of partnerships for international aid and development has become ubiquitous, and their value has been too-little questioned. In the area of education, Francine Menashy's book remedies this with a detailed, probing analysis of such partnerships in theory and practice.

Partnerships have become enshrined in the international development literature. In 2000, one of the United Nations (UN) Millennium Development Goals (MDGs) was devoted to the role of partnerships. In the same era, the World Bank and the International Monetary Fund (IMF) were forced to shift their approach from structural adjustment programs (SAPs) to poverty reduction strategy processes (PRSPs). One of the hallmarks of PRSPs was their intent to promote widespread participation by and partnership with all stakeholders, including governments, other aid agencies, civil society organizations (CSOs), the private sector, and the poor themselves. Indeed, this call for participation and partnership is one of the key features in the search for something to replace the neoliberal SAPs that underpin the so-called Washington Consensus. Partnerships have become even more central to the 2015 UN Sustainable Development Goals (SDGs). The United Nations envisions a global partnership of all these stakeholders to "work in a spirit of global solidarity, in particular solidarity with the poorest and with people in vulnerable situations" (quoted in Menashy, p. 1).

Has this emphasis on partnerships for international development worked? Made a difference? Not very much, in my view. Despite ubiquitous partnerships, none of the MDGs were achieved by 2015 (those who say that the reduction in extreme poverty was achieved use a very inadequate measure of extreme poverty). The SDGs have simply postponed achieving them until 2030, and, at the moment, the 17 2030 goals don't look very achievable. PRSPs have generated very limited degrees of participation and partnership, and the results look a lot like SAPs. One fundamental problem is with the oft-touted principle of country ownership of development strategies. Partnerships are supposed to be led by the country that is affected. But the Global North countries provide finance to recipient countries from the Global South, so partnerships are always unbalanced and far from country owned (Menashy explores the complexity of these partnerships). PRSPs illustrate the problem; the World Bank and the IMF have created a 1,200-page manual on how to do a PRSP, making country ownership a pipe dream.

One of the major facets of the discussion of partnerships in recent years is faith in working with the private sector. Public–private partnerships (PPPs) have been seen as the answer to a shortage of public funds for development and as a source of know-how for problem solving. But to me, the private sector is too self-interested and unaccustomed to dealing with knotty social problems that are not well defined and have no optimal solution. In a past life, I was a student at Stanford University's Graduate School of Business. There, I had a professor who wrote a paper entitled "The Social Responsibility of Business and Other Pollutants of the Air." He was pro-business. His point was that the business of business was business. Corporate philanthropy or trying to form partnerships that align public needs with business interests is not likely to be very successful. The current effort to get the private sector to partner with the public sector in "impact investing" in social programs is unlikely to yield much: it will likely mobilize few resources, and it will distort all projects toward a few measurable outcomes.

Most fundamentally, the idea of partnership posits a harmonious world in which we are all in this together, trying to solve our social problems. While I am not questioning the motives of the people involved, we live in a world where our very structures reproduce and maintain inequalities. Saying that all partners will "work in a spirit of . . . solidarity with the poorest" hides or ignores the very structures under which, for example, private-sector interests are quite different from those of the most vulnerable.

This is not to say partnerships have no place in development policy and practice. In the future, we will need unprecedented cooperation and coordination, from the local level to the global, simply to survive, let alone progress. Such change can be furthered by new partnerships, but not based on unexamined assumptions, or, worse still, some idealized, warm and fuzzy "let's get together" idea. The concept of partnership, as generally used today, misses and actually negates the dissent, struggle, and collective action that are necessary to transform fundamentally unequal, unfair, and often oppressive relations into partnerships of mutuality, reciprocity, and fairness.

While I have been raising issues generally about partnerships in international development, Menashy focuses on these issues and more as they apply to aid to education. Her trenchant and meticulous examination of partnerships in education recognizes their promise, but shows how power dynamics too often yield problematic results. The case studies of the Global Partnership for Education (GPE) and the Education Cannot Wait Fund (ECW) are important in their own right as global partnerships aimed at some of the most serious education problems we face. While her analysis is quite critical of partnerships as presently constituted, Menashy ends with some valuable suggestions to improve them.

—*Steven J. Klees*

Acknowledgments

I am so very grateful to the many individuals who have generously offered input on my research over the years and who gave critiques and suggestions on drafts of this book. I wish to thank the following supportive colleagues who read sections of the manuscript and provided enormously valuable and thoughtful feedback: Sarah Dryden-Peterson, Moira Faul, Meggan Madden, Caroline Manion, Karen Mundy, Robin Shields, and Zeena Zakharia. Of these, I am particularly grateful to Robin and Zeena, who each very generously agreed to allow me to use data in this book that we collected and analyzed collaboratively. A special thanks to my "writing groupies," Avary Carhill-Poza and Gerardo Blanco, who offered support and guidance throughout the book-writing process. My work has benefited tremendously from the research assistance of my past and current students, including Karen Crounse, Sheetal Gowda, and Alvine Sangang. I owe a huge thank-you to Emily Woods, who helped in the preparation and editing of the final manuscript. Thank you to my wonderful colleagues in the Leadership in Education Department at University of Massachusetts Boston, and I am particularly grateful to my department chair, Tara Parker, and Dean Joe Berger for their ongoing support of my work.

Sections of this book detail findings of studies that benefited from a Spencer Foundation/National Academy of Education Postdoctoral Fellowship; a research grant from Education International; and a Joseph P. Healey Grant from UMass Boston. Parts of the book were previously published in the *Journal of Education Policy*; *Globalisation, Societies, and Education*; and *Comparative Education* (all used with permission). I wish to thank the editors of these journals and the anonymous reviewers of the articles, which were truly improved through the peer-review process.

Thank you to all those at Teachers College Press for your support throughout the publishing process, and to Gita Steiner-Khamsi for including this book in the series on *International Perspectives on Educational Reform*. I wish to express sincere appreciation to Steve Klees for contributing such an insightful foreword to the book

I am grateful to the interview respondents, who graciously gave their time and insights. In particular, I thank those who agreed to follow-up interviews years later to ensure the validity and current relevance of the findings.

To my mom and dad, and my sister Debrah, I am lucky to have such an incredible family. To Ella and Leo, you are the best, I love you so much, and I thank you for helping me see perspective on life and for always making me laugh. And most of all, thank you to my wonderful husband, Aaron. I could not have written a word of this book without your unwavering encouragement, patience, sense of humor, and kindness.

List of Abbreviations

AUSAID	Australian Agency for International Development
BCG	Boston Consulting Group
CGIAR	Consultative Group for International Agricultural Research
CSO	civil society organization
CSR	corporate social responsibility
DANIDA	Danish International Development Agency
DCP	developing country partner
DfID	Department for International Development (United Kingdom)
ECW	Education Cannot Wait
EFA	Education for All
EOF	Education Outcomes Fund for Africa and the Middle East
FTI	Fast Track Initiative
GAVI	Global Alliance for Vaccines and Immunization
GBC-E	Global Business Coalition for Education
GCE	Global Campaign for Education
GIZ	Deutsche Gesellschaft für Internationale Zusammenarbeit (German Development Agency)
GPE	Global Partnership for Education
HLSG	High-Level Steering Group
IEFG	International Education Funders Group
IEI	Inclusive Education Initiative
IFFEd	International Financing Facility for Education
IGO	Intergovernmental organization
INEE	Inter-Agency Network for Education in Emergencies
INGO	International nongovernmental organization
IO	international organization

IWGE	International Working Group on Education
LEG	Local Education Group
MDGs	Millennium Development Goals
MSP	Multistakeholder Partnership
NGO	nongovernment organization
OCHA	United Nations Office for the Coordination of Humanitarian Affairs
ODA	Overseas Development Assistance
ODI	Overseas Development Institute
OECD	Organisation for Economic Co-Operation and Development
OECD DAC	Organisation for Economic Co-Operation and Development, Development Assistance Committee
PPP	public–private partnership
SAP	structural adjustment program
SIDA	Swedish International Development Cooperation Agency
SDGs	Sustainable Development Goals
UN	United Nations
UNDP	United Nations Development Programme
UNESCO	United Nations Educational, Scientific, and Cultural Organization
UNICEF	United Nations Children's Fund
UNGEI	United Nations Girls' Education Initiative
USAID	United States Agency for International Development
WHS	World Humanitarian Summit

CHAPTER 1

Introduction

Conceptualizing Power in an Era of Partnerships

In August 2015, then-United Nations (UN) secretary-general Ban Ki-moon announced to the world that member states had reached agreement on the Sustainable Development Goals (SDGs)—an ambitious and noble agenda to "free the human race from the tyranny of poverty" by 2030 (UN, 2015a). A total of 17 separate thematic areas, grounded in the principles of human rights, equality, and sustainability, had been selected as core goals. With an overarching aim of poverty eradication, the SDGs, according to Ban, "fully [integrate] the economic, social, and environmental dimensions of sustainable development and calls for action by all countries, poor, rich and middle-income" (UN, 2015b). As a successor to and expansion of the 8 Millennium Development Goals (MDGs), which ended in 2015, the 17 SDG goals and 169 targets cover an expansive set of social, economic, and environmental issues, ranging from hunger, health, and gender equity to climate change, water, energy, and urbanization.

Many scholars, practitioners, and policy actors from the field of education are likely most familiar with SDG number 4, on Quality Education— namely, to "ensure inclusive and equitable quality education and promote lifelong learning opportunities for all" (UN, 2015c). My focus throughout this book, however, most relates to the last of the SDGs, number 17: "Partnerships for the Goals," which aims to "strengthen the means of implementation and revitalize the global partnership for sustainable development" (UNDP, 2018). The UN resolution *Transforming Our World: The 2030 Agenda for Sustainable Development* places partnership at the core of the SDGs and their successful implementation:

> This Partnership will work in a spirit of global solidarity, in particular solidarity with the poorest and with people in vulnerable situations. It will facilitate an intensive global engagement in support of implementation of all the Goals and targets, bringing together Governments, the private sector, civil society, the United Nations system and other actors and mobilizing all available resources. (UN, 2015c, p. 10)

According to the resolution, the rest of the SDGs are dependent on number 17—they can only be achieved through partnership.

When established in 2000, the MDGs also sought to forge partnerships. But according to a UN system task team on the post-2015 agenda, the MDG number 8 goal, "To develop a global partnership for development," was not achieved due to several shortcomings in both design and implementation. Most notably, it "perpetuated a 'donor-recipient' type of relationship and did not pay sufficient attention to mobilizing development financing other than aid" (UN, 2013, p. v). As the task team advised:

> A renewed global partnership should aim at making international arrangements for collective decision-making and corresponding government policies that can meet the challenges at hand. This will require a partnership at the global level between all groupings of countries, multilateral organizations and other stake-holders. (UN, 2013, p. 10)

The term *partnerships*, according to these statements, suggests positive, cooperative, collaborative, equitable, and inclusive relationships among all actors, from the Global North and Global South and from the state and nonstate sectors. Partnerships, moreover, can allow the mobilization of new, nontraditional funding sources for development. As I show in this book, a partnership-based mandate for development was first proposed long before the SDGs, and this agenda remains pervasive throughout all sectors of international development and aid, including education. And as reflected in the SDGs, as well as in several other global mandates and declarations, partnerships explicitly respond to past critiques of the aid architecture—reproached as being northern-driven, undemocratic, and dismissive of southern, local participation.

A widely held ideal underpins this trend toward partnership: Through collaborative efforts, power imbalances can shift, making international educational development more just. This book questions whether these efforts have in fact produced such a shift in power. I ask: Can partnerships truly ameliorate power imbalances, or do they reproduce and exacerbate the inequities they are meant to address? This book explores the changing nature of aid to education and power dynamics via case studies of recent partnership initiatives. It systematically shows how efforts to engender a more participatory aid architecture and increase country ownership have primarily solidified the power of actors from the Global North, in particular international organizations such as the World Bank, UNICEF, bilateral donors, and the private sector.

I examine power dynamics within partnership arrangements through three lenses. First, the network created through partnership-based organizations exposes a structure that reinforces hierarchical aid relationships. Second, power is understood through a case study of the most prominent multistakeholder agency in education, the Global Partnership for Education (GPE), where northern actors are shown to wield the most influence. And third is the case of the Education Cannot Wait Fund (ECW)—a humanitarian fund for education in emergencies, which shows similar North/South dynamics. Both GPE and ECW, moreover, highlight the rise of private-sector actors as key partners holding legitimacy in global education policy circles.

In this introductory chapter, I provide ways of conceptualizing *partnership*, which, although I place it as a core theme in this book, poses some challenges in terms of presenting a concrete definition. I also offer a conceptual understanding of *power* and a framework developed by international relations scholars Michael Barnett and Raymond Duvall, which informs my analysis. I then give an overview of methodological approaches and data collected for the research presented, including social network analysis and process tracing. And I offer notes on some of the terminology used, such as *aid, Global North,* and *Global South.* This introduction also provides a rationale for this book, acknowledges some limitations, and previews the remaining chapters.

UNDERSTANDING PARTNERSHIP

Intuitively, we all likely hold a particular definition of partnership that applies accurately to our own relationships with others, both personally and in professional practice. And in most cases, our definitions likely elicit overwhelmingly positive associations. Similarly, rhetoric relating to partnerships in global policy mandates, as well as in development practices, connotes positive relationships, in which two or more actors join together to accomplish something desirable.

In reality, the definition of partnership in international development remains somewhat unclear. The term is cloaked in ambiguity, and few can definitively state "what the idea of partnership is actually supposed to mean . . . partnership remains an impoverished theoretical appeal, which is under-defined, poorly scrutinised and rather unconvincingly utilised as a guiding concept in applied practice" (Barnes & Brown, 2011, p. 166). Similarly, Crawford (2003, p. 142) notes that partnership's "common usage . . . leads to both multiple interpretations and a lack of definitional clarity." The vague definition of the term *partnership* allows a range of interpretations, and this malleability might be considered either a weakness or a strength. On the one hand, a vague concept makes its application very challenging and oftentimes unhelpful, or even "misleading" (Adams & Martens, 2016, p. 2). But on the other hand, as I'll explain in more detail in Chapter 2, a degree of malleability has allowed the idea to be picked up by a diverse set of actors for a range of purposes.

Some of the most common interpretations of partnership are fundamentally practical, simply alluding to working well together to arrive at mutually positive results. Partnerships, in this sense, embody such elements as coordination, collaboration, coalitions for action, reciprocity between actors and organizations, and joining together "diverse approaches, structures, and purposes," and yet with a common pragmatic, instrumentalist aim (OCED, 2015, p. 17; also see Barnes, Brown, & Harman, 2016; Faul, 2016a; Lister, 2000).

As it relates to international development and aid, this practical conceptualization of partnership is widespread, implying that collective activities will arguably lead to more effective development practices. It is argued that partnerships help reduce issues of duplication and fragmentation through more coordinated efforts. At the same time, when agencies and governments partner, the monitoring of development programs increases in effectiveness. Partnerships allow information sharing, knowledge mobilization, broader policy dialogue, and collective responsibility for success. In more recent years, partnership has taken on notions of economic risk-sharing. The Organisation for Economic Co-operation and Development (OECD) explains that "partnerships are powerful drivers of development" (OECD, 2015, p. 17). Some partnerships are considered tidy, in which partners have much in common. Arguably more common in international development are instead what Guijt (2010, p. 1028) describes as "messy partnerships," where partners are drawn together because of a common vision or mandate, but each with its own unique means of communication, decisionmaking, degree of influence, and capacity to act.

Much of the partnership rhetoric in international development makes clear that key partners must be those on the receiving end of aid, which include beneficiary countries, predominantly those in the Global South, that are often termed *southern, community,* or *local participation.* This related concept of participation has been described as a "buzzword" in international development that "can be used to evoke—and to signify—almost anything that involves people. As such, it can easily be reframed to meet almost any demand made of it" (Cornwall, 2008, p. 269). Scholars have offered various typologies to describe different forms of participation, often on a continuum. These include "tokenized" representation, with little influence; "functional" participation, in which partners are included to achieve objectives in efficient ways; "representative" participation, making space for all partner voices; and "transformative" participation, with a goal of empowerment for all partners (Cornwall, 2008, pp. 270–272).[1] The Inter-Agency Network for Education in Emergencies (INEE) distinguishes between "symbolic" and "active" or "full" participation, the latter involving "the active contribution of time and direct involvement in decision-making, planning and implementation of education activities" (INEE, 2010, p. 20). As will be unpacked throughout this book, most partnerships rhetorically present participation as active, connecting to a related concept: country ownership.

Country ownership implies that governments and local actors themselves must be at the helm of policy decisions on aid to their own countries. International aid policy frames country ownership as occurring when recipients of aid "take ownership of development policies and aid activities in their country, to establish their own systems for coordinating donors, and only to accept aid that suits their needs" (de Renzio, Whitfield, & Bergamaschi, 2008, p. 1). Defined as such, country ownership is widely considered a primary tenet to a broader mandate of partnership in international development.

Practical considerations underpin these notions of partnership as inclusive of southern, recipient actors, embracing notions of full participation and country ownership. Most notably, through partnerships, aid policies and programs can be designed in a more contextual way, leading to increased effectiveness. The INEE explains that "community participation in assessment, planning, implementation, management and monitoring helps to ensure that education responses are appropriate and effective" (INEE, 2010, p. 20).

Another interpretation, often presented parallel to this pragmatic-based definition, applies a normative conceptualization of partnership. In this sense, *partnership* implies a transformative rearrangement of relationships, underpinned by equity. Scholars have applied elements of distributive justice theory to better understand partnerships in this normative sense, in particular relating to distributions of benefits, equitable representation, and opportunities for participation in legitimate decisionmaking processes (Barnes & Brown, 2011). As Fowler (2000, p. 3) describes: "Authentic partnership implies, inter alia, a joint commitment to long-term interaction, shared responsibility for achievement, reciprocal obligation, equality, mutuality and balance of power." Partnerships in this way are transformative, empowering those actors who have traditionally occupied lower tiers in the aid hierarchy through active participation and ownership.

In the aid arena, agencies have embraced this normative connotation of partnership as well. For example, the Organisation for Economic Co-Operation and Development, Development Assistance Committee (OECD DAC) made one of the earliest appeals to a partnership-based mandate when it stated: "Paternalistic approaches have no place in this framework. In a true partnership, local actors should progressively take the lead while external partners back their efforts to assume greater responsibility for their own development" (OECD, 1996, p. 13). Country ownership reflects more than just increased effectiveness through contextualized interventions, but an embracing of local actors' rights to engage in the development decisions that directly affect them. Under this conceptualization, "aid relationships have been recast as partnerships between donor and recipient countries, with donors attesting that they no longer seek to impose their vision of development on poor countries but instead wish to be partners in strategies determined and 'owned' by recipients themselves" (Abrahamsen, 2004, p. 1453).

As will be discussed in Chapter 2, the partnership mandate in development arose in part to respond to the widely critiqued standard of top-down aid policies, transforming the rhetoric, where "governments, along with domestic NGOs and local community-level actors, were to form partnerships in the process of developing their own poverty reduction strategies. As a result, 'country ownership' became a key word in international development" (Vavrus & Seghers, 2010, p. 85). A partnership, in this sense, "prioritizes the social logic of inclusion and participation of traditionally marginalized social actors in partnerships" (Faul, 2016a, p. 3). This normative conception of partnership, therefore, reflects a redistribution of power from the Global North to the Global South (Barnes et al., 2016; Crawford, 2003; Fowler, 2000).

As reflected in the SDGs and several other mandates, partnership as conceptualized in international aid, and aid to education in particular, often conflates with the narrower term *public–private partnership (PPP)* because most global partnerships explicitly involve nonstate actors, including foundations and companies. Partnership as involving the private sector reflects the participation of business actors as much as donors and recipients. As will also be discussed in Chapter 2, largely driven by a push to "mobilize private investment" (OECD, 2015, p. 27), through philanthropy and corporate social responsibility (CSR), the development lexicon increasingly adopts the term *partnership* as code for engagement of the private sector (Fengler & Kharas, 2011; Utting & Zammit, 2009).

Rooted in both practical and normative foundations, partnership is a foundational concept throughout this book, and I question its very malleable and broad definition in application to global partnerships in education.

UNDERSTANDING POWER

Just as we all likely hold an intuitive definition of *partnership*, the concept of *power* tends to elicit particular thoughts based on our own beliefs and experiences. As a conventional definition, power is characterized by "the capacities of actors to determine the conditions of their existence" (Barnett & Duvall, 2005a, p. 42) or "the ability of people to achieve what they want" (Hunjan & Pettit, 2011, p. 5). I present power, however, as a more nuanced concept, given that the action of holding power, or not, and the implications of this, differ depending on context and the standpoint of analysis. Scholarship on international relations has conceptualized power in a variety of ways, focusing not only on the traditional notions of asymmetries between states in military strength or resources, but also on the influence of information, ideas, or so-called soft power, such as culture and religion (Finnemore & Sikkink, 2001; Keohane, 2006; Nye, 2004).

An analysis of power must not only identify its existence, but also question in what ways power is exercised, or "how, why, and when some actors have 'power over' others" (Barnett & Duvall, 2005b, p. 2). To explain power dynamics in partnership-based environments, this book employs a conceptual framework that not only examines which actors have power over others, but also how power is produced, retained, and reinforced; in other words, how some actors are empowered while others are not. I apply the theoretical "taxonomy of power" developed by international relations scholars Barnett and Duvall (2005a, 2005b), who identify four forms of power: (1) compulsory power, (2) institutional power, (3) structural power, and (4) productive power. I primarily use structural power and productive power to analyze and understand global educational partnerships.

The most commonly invoked conception of power in the study of international relations and development is *compulsory power*, which "is best understood as the ability of A to get B to do what B otherwise would not do [and] there is intentionality on the part of Actor A" (Barnett & Duvall, 2005a, p. 49). When compulsory power is enacted due to a conflict of desires, Actor B is compelled to change and abide by the desires of Actor A, and "A is successful because it has material and ideational resources at its disposal that lead B to alter its actions" (p. 49).

While compulsory power works through direct conflict, *institutional power* "exists in actors' indirect control over the conditions of action of socially distant others" (Barnett & Duvall, 2005a, p. 48). Institutional power is enacted through indirect avenues, where agendas and associated rules allow actors to control others, and where weaker actors have less of a say in the adoption of such agendas. Between Actors A and B are formal and informal institutions that determine the relationship among the two through procedures and rules: "In other words, A does not 'possess' the resources of power, but because A stands in a particular relation to the relevant institutional arrangements, its actions exercise power over B" (Barnett & Duvall, 2005a, p. 51). As Barnett and Finnemore argue, in international development, institutional power manifests not in direct conflicts, but in "the way international organizations [IOs] can exercise power through their agenda-setting activities . . . IO staff frequently have the formal and informal capacity to determine the agenda at fora, meetings, and conferences. This capacity gives them a substantial role in determining what is—and what is not—discussed" (2005, p. 177). Although not applied in detail in this book, I do note in Chapter 2 the ways in which compulsory power and institutional power have been enacted in educational development—namely, through aid conditionalities and the Education for All (EFA) mandate.

Structural power concerns the social positionality of actors within a structure and how this position then determines their capacities and interests. In focusing on structure, analyses of power examine actors' locations in a hierarchy. Within this hierarchical structure, actors, their capacities, and their interests are being constituted through interactions with one another. Barnett and Duvall argue that structural power is exhibited when "the social relational capacities, subjectivities, and interests of actors are directly shaped by the social position that they occupy" (Barnett & Duvall, 2005b, pp. 18–20). Structural power, moreover, is historically constituted: "structures—including structures of domination—have histories; they are (re)produced or transformed only through the mediation of historically concrete agency" (Rupert, 2005, p. 209). Therefore, power can be perpetuated in international development through such factors as colonial legacies, the maintenance of past aid distribution re-lationships, and the retaining of actors' longstanding responsibilities in such areas as administration, implementation, and governance. Structural power is reinforced through the preservation of economic roles that are constructed and conceptualized in relation to one another—for instance, donor and recipient roles are indicative of mutually constituted capacities, where structural posi-tion A (the recipient country) exists only in relation to position B (the donor country) (Barnett & Duvall, 2005b, p.18).

Deeply embedded in these structures, actors may moreover be unable to recognize their own exercise of power, nor their subordination and op-pression: "To the degree that it does, actors' self-understandings and dispo-sitions for action serve to reproduce, rather than to resist, the differential capacities and privileges of structure" (Barnett & Duvall, 2005a, p. 53). Through this hegemonic reproduction of asymmetries, structural power "substantially determines the capacities and resources of actors" (Barnett & Duvall, 2005a, p. 20). As Naylor (2011) applies structural power, it "cocon-stitutes actors within hierarchical structures in which certain actors are de-fined as dominant and empowered with greater resources and capacities for action, and other actors are simultaneously constituted as submissive and disempowered with limited resources and capacities for action" (p. 183).

In educational aid, structural power is arguably reproduced through the maintenance of established international financing arrangements and actor positions within this hierarchical aid architecture. This book exposes such a hierarchy within the global educational aid network, and also more spe-cifically, within the GPE and ECW, where the structure of aid to education has shaped the capacities of its partners to steer decisionmaking and argu-ably has reproduced traditional international development power dynamics within and across partnerships.

Similar to structural power, *productive power* enacts through "constitu-tive social processes" in which actors' identities, interests, and positionality are socially produced (Barnett & Duvall, 2005a, p. 55). But in the productive sense, power instead operates through discursive practices, legitimating only particular forms of knowledge. Productive power works through general-ized discourse that applies to all actors and "defines what constitutes legiti-mate knowledge, and shapes whose knowledge matters" (Barnett & Duvall, 2005b, p. 4).

While structural power attends to hierarchical relationships and the ways in which some actors are advantaged and empowered within a particular structure, productive power works through "changing understandings, meanings, norms, customs, and social identities that make possible, limit, and are drawn on for action" (Barnett & Duvall, 2005a, p. 56). Productive power, therefore, is applied to how actors and their positions are discursively produced and legitimated: "Productive power concerns discourse, the social processes and the systems of knowledge through which meaning is produced, fixed, lived, experienced, and transformed. . . . Thus to attend to the analysis of productive power is to focus on how diffuse and contingent social processes produce particular kinds of subjects, fix meanings and categories, and create what is taken for granted and the ordinary of world politics" (pp. 55–57).

Productive power constructs what actors perceive as reality, with signifying ideas taken for granted as permanent and normalized. For example, terms such as *developing, fragile, vulnerable,* and *marginalized,* in relation to particular actors or states, denote readily accepted and natural understandings of the world and people, as though fixed (Barnett & Duvall, 2005a; Naylor, 2011).

As this book details, the roles of private actors have been discursively constituted through broad and taken-for-granted narratives, readily normalized, embraced, and applied across the education and development arena and clearly evidenced in the rhetoric surrounding multistakeholder partnerships (MSPs), including, for example, the discourses of *technical expertise, innovative, efficient, creative,* and *nontraditional,* all playing into the definition of what constitutes a legitimate policy actor. I propose that scholars and practitioners might view MSPs as producing a particular conception of the private sector, which in turn benefits from this productive power—namely, the diffusion of discourse that, as Finnemore (2014, p. 223) describes, is "deployed to *create* these new actors" as key players in development. Partnerships, in this sense, work to constitute a particular educational aid arena that "is productive of particular kinds of actors and associate practices" (Barnett & Finnemore, 2005, p. 179).

Those familiar with constructivist theory may find the concepts of structural and productive power familiar, given that each aligns with the well-known works of Gill and Law (1989) and Cox (1992). World systems theory also speaks to aspects of structural power, where positionality in the world system (core, semiperiphery, periphery) defines the identities and interests of actors (and states) (Barnett & Duvall, 2005a; Wallerstein, 2004). Michel Foucault's conceptions of subject and power also inform understandings of the co-constitutive nature of structural and productive power, where "power relations are rooted deep in the social nexus, not reconstituted 'above' society as a supplementary structure" (Foucault, 1982, p. 791). In the study of global governance and international aid, from a constructivist standpoint, "the realities of the global are socially produced" (Muppidi, 2005, p. 274).

I have chosen to focus on only two forms of power in this book, but I must note that compulsory and institutional power still operate in education and development. My application of mainly structural and productive power rests on their constructivist underpinnings, where both forms "work through social relations of constitution" and therefore apply clearly not only to partnership organizations, but also to the wide network of all actors. Barnett and Duvall's framework speaks readily to the phenomena exposed through my research. First, my findings show how, despite changes in rhetoric and practice and (as stated frequently by interview respondents) the "best of intentions," inequities in education and development partnership spaces persist within a hierarchical structure. At the same time, I observe that a new group of actors has been increasingly legitimized and empowered within partnerships, based on a particular discourse surrounding their roles and rationalizing their engagement.

As Naylor (2011, p. 183) aptly describes, Barnett and Duvall's framework befits a deeper understanding of power dynamics in international education:

> [T]his multifaceted definition of power points to an asymmetry and an inequality in the international system. Ideationally and materially, certain actors inhabit superior positions that empower them to set not only their own policies and agendas but also those of others. Their positions also allow them to discursively influence the structure of the system itself and in doing so to (re)constitute actors and their abilities. That is, the system allows for certain actors to have an asymmetric capacity to "define or be defined."

METHODS AND DATA COLLECTED

This book reflects the results of applying two key methodological approaches: network analysis and process-tracing analysis. These quantitative and qualitative methods, which were applied to different data sets, each sought to understand power in global education and partnerships through different forms of analysis. I explain each of them next, as well as the ways that these methodological approaches have been applied in this book.

Social Network Analysis

Social network analysis has been primarily applied in Chapter 3, and it reflects research that I conducted collaboratively with Dr. Robin Shields of the University of Bath. Chapter 3 examines a unique data set of the membership of seven partnership-based organizations in education: the Global Campaign for Education (GCE); the INEE; the United Nations Girls

Education Initiative (UNGEI); the Global Partnership for Education; the United Nations Global Education First Initiative; the Global Business Coalition for Education (GBC-E); and the International Working Group on Education (IWGE). These seven organizations were selected based on their prominence in the field of educational development and included as those that describe their structure as an equal partnership; include state and non-state representation; target education as a global issue affecting cross-border populations; and have the mandate to improve educational access, quality, or both in the Global South, although with a range of foci, including advocacy, financing, policy design, knowledge sharing, and program development. For each partnership included, the membership lists were publicly available, retrieved from organizational websites.

The membership of these organizations totaled 293 separate entities, with each entity holding membership in between one and five partnerships. The entities were then classified by type: civil society/nongovernmental organizations (NGOs), bilateral donors, international organizations, recipient governments, foundations, businesses, and research institutes. Entities were also classified into either "Northern" or "Southern," based on whether it was located in a high-, middle-, or low-income country (a discussion of the North/South distinction made in this book follows). The entities and their relationships were then explored by using the Google Geocoding application programming interface to situate each entity at a more precise geospatial coordinate, producing visualizations of the global structure of the network through a geographic plot (see Figure 3.1).

From the lists of memberships, we created an affiliation network—a network in which the strength of a tie between two organizations is the number of common memberships they hold in the seven partnership-based organizations (Borgatti & Halgin, 2011). Thus, if two entities are both members in two common partnerships, the strength of the tie between them would be two. Similarly, if two organizations do not share membership in any partnership-based organization, they are not connected to one another in the network. Social network analysis methods examined the network (Wasserman & Faust 1994), and in this book, I focus mainly on measures of degree centrality. *Degree centrality* is a count of the connections, or "ties," to each actor in the network, and it "is often interpreted in terms of the potential power that an actor might wield due to the ability to slow down flows or to distort what is passed along in such a way as to serve the actor's interests" (Borgatti, Mehra, Brass, & Labianca, 2009, p. 894). Using linear regression models, the centrality of entities in the network was found as an outcome of the type of organization and its location's income level, specifically testing the proposition that centrality differs between Northern and Southern countries when controlling for the type of organization.

As I explain in much detail in Chapter 3, network analysis methodologies are particularly suitable for the themes I explore throughout this book, including *hypercollective action*, which involves a transformation in the overall aid environment to include new and different types of actors that converge in multiple spaces (Severino & Ray, 2010). Network analysis, as will be shown, also allows the exploration of different forms of power and exposes, through quantitative methods, power dynamics in the global education arena through the lens of partnerships.

Process Tracing

In Chapters 4 and 5, I present case studies of the GPE and the ECW, respectively, and apply process-tracing methods. Sections of the research for Chapter 5, particularly as relating to private-sector participation in ECW, are based on data I collected collaboratively with Dr. Zeena Zakharia of the University of Massachusetts Boston. Process tracing occurs within a case study and "is an analytic tool for drawing descriptive and causal inferences from diagnostic pieces of evidence—often understood as part of a temporal sequence of events or phenomena" (Bennett, 2010; Collier, 2011, p.824). Described as a "within case analysis," process tracing often targets policymaking and policymakers (Tansey, 2007; Vennesson, 2008, p. 235). Through process tracing, I sought to understand the processes that resulted in the GPE's and ECW's governance structure, strategic planning, distribution of responsibilities, policymaking procedures, and implementation practices, with an overarching aim to determine influence and power dynamics.

To support the process-tracing analyses, in order to understand particular events, viewpoints and processes, and the perspectives of key actors involved, data include 56 key informant elite interviews. Elite interviews provide firsthand accounts from "significant players," or participants directly involved in the historical events and circumstances associated with the case being studied (Bennett, 2010; Tansey, 2007). The goal of elite interviewing within process tracing is not to arrive at generalizable conclusions from a random sample of respondents, but instead "to obtain the testimony of individuals who were most closely involved in the process of interest" (Tansey, 2007, pp. 767–768). Via purposive sampling, to gain an understanding of the perspectives of various stakeholders who were able to speak to any historical shifts and more recent activities of GPE and ECW, respondents were explicitly selected based on their current or past role within the organization's governance (i.e., the board of directors or High-Level Steering Group [HLSG]), the Secretariats, in-country grant management, partner organizations, and expert advisors. Representatives of bilateral donor agencies, United Nations/multilateral agencies, civil society organizations/nongovernmental organizations (CSOs/ NGOs), recipient/beneficiary countries, foundations, businesses, and independent respondents were interviewed.[2] See Table 1.1 for a breakdown of interview respondents. Several respondents spoke to experiences in both GPE

Table 1.1. Key Informants Interviewed

Key Informant	Number
United Nations/multilateral agency	5
Northern civil society/nongovernment organization	9
Southern civil society/nongovernment organization	8
Recipient/beneficiary	7
Bilateral donor	6
MSP Secretariat	7
Foundation	4
Business	7
Independent	3
Total	56

and ECW, given that (as described in Chapter 3) comembership in partnerships is quite common.

Interviews lasted between 25 and 90 minutes, with an average length of roughly one hour. All interviews were transcribed and coded. Key informant interviews took place over a 4-year span, from 2014 to 2018. Given the time gap between some of the earlier interviews and the publication of this book, I followed up with 10 key informants interviewed in 2014 and 2015 who agreed to participate in follow-up conversations, primarily to determine if any of their experiences or viewpoints had changed, and I have updated findings where applicable.

The interviews cited in this book have been coded to ensure the anonymity of respondents. Therefore, I apply very general codes as identifiers based on either the type of organization the respondent represented or as a Secretariat staff member.[3] All data collection involving human subjects was conducted after approval by my university's institutional review board. All interview respondents provided informed consent to participating and audio-recording, and all identifying information has been kept strictly confidential.

The process tracing was also supported by analyses of over 200 publicly available organizational documents from GPE, ECW, and their partner organizations, including minutes of meetings, final reports of meetings, strategic plans, background papers, commissioned research, and promotional materials. Social media and websites were also included in the analysis. All documents were accessed online, with the exception of one report emailed directly to me by an interview respondent.

Although I focus on two organizations in the process tracing, my findings do not reflect direct engagement or observation of GPE and ECW meetings or Secretariat activities, and so I base my analysis on only public written materials and anonymous key informant interviews.

Although treated as distinct analyses in separate chapters of this book, in the concluding chapter, I compare the network analysis and process tracings and discuss the ways in which the findings complement each other, allowing similar and reinforcing conclusions.

NOTES ON TERMINOLOGY

Defining *Aid*

A term frequently applied in this book is international *aid*. As Riddell (2007) describes, in its broadest terms, aid "consists of all resources—physical goods, skills and technical know-how, financial grants (gifts), or loans (at concessional rates)—transferred from donors to recipients" (p. 17). Yet, as Riddell points out, this definition does not adequately capture many of aid's complexities and nuances, including who the donors and recipients are, the reasons why they give or receive aid, and the impacts of aid. Neither does a broad definition capture the differences between certain purposes of aid. For instance, *development aid* or *development assistance* generally means resources from high-income countries to support projects and programs to help accelerate economic or social development within low-income countries and directed to those in poverty (Riddell, 2007). The OECD defines aid as flowing from governments to governments, referred to as *Overseas Development Assistance (ODA)*, but this notably falls short, as it excludes any resources from, or to, nonstate actors. Aid in the current environment can come from a very wide range of sources, including the traditional state-based governments and multilaterals, but also from nonstate-sector sources such as religious organizations, charities, NGOs, foundations (also termed *philanthropies*), and businesses. As well, aid sometimes can flow from North to South, or South to South. And aid sometimes flows within countries, where national actors provide resources to assist fellow citizens in need, which can be seen occurring in both northern and southern contexts. The term *humanitarian aid* more specifically captures resources deployed to respond to humanitarian crises and emergencies (Ramalingam, 2013; Riddell, 2007).

When particular forms of aid are not distinguished from each other, my understanding (and the definition I use in this book) is quite broad, where international aid to education means resources flowing from any source (state or nonstate) to support education within countries in need, often characterized as low income, in the Global South, and supplying resources for those experiencing emergencies, including governments, but also individual people, such as refugees or those internally displaced.

Global North and Global South

Throughout this book, I apply the distinction of *Global North* and *Global South*—terminology often both critiqued and embraced, and defined in different ways. First, I wish to acknowledge some of the indisputable shortcomings of the distinction. The clearest issue with Global North/Global South relates to the fact that this geographic distinction makes little sense. As Magallanes (2015) explains: "Despite the advantages this designation offers as a synthesizing term, I consider it ambiguous because it uses a simple geographical criteria to describe a complex social situation which distinguishes poor countries from the wealthiest" (p. 8). This ambiguity elicits confusion, particularly when the distinction is interpreted as ignoring what is commonly and instinctively viewed as a characteristic of the Global South, but that in fact also occurs within the Global North—for instance, sites of extreme poverty within the United States, often depicted as the richest country in the world (Kaltmeier, 2015, p. 10). In this sense, the idea of "the South in the North" is somewhat oxymoronic. The North/South concept, moreover, gives the impression of an easily observed global binary, split in two, when the world is plainly much more complex.

However, while acknowledging these shortcomings and the imperfections of this terminology, I choose to apply the North/South distinction for the following reasons. First, I believe that most other options are problematic. One traditionally and commonly used term would likely be *Third World*, which made sense only in reference to a past geopolitical world that also included so-called First World capitalist economies and Second World communist countries. Upon the end of the Cold War, these distinctions were no longer relevant. Another common binary that continues to be used is *developed* and *developing* countries. I personally take issue with this framing because, as Clarke (2018) explains, the distinction implies some problematic assumptions, including "the narrow focus it entailed on economic growth and levels of industrialisation; the assumption that 'development' would help so-called 'traditional societies' catch-up with 'modern ones' (modernisation theory); the implication that there was a universal measurement of 'development' and that national development could be assessed against this (western) standard; and, the assumption of linear progress. In addition to other problems, this division of the world projected a similar future for all nations." The idea that countries are "developing" reflects an evolutionary perspective, where all countries are on the same path to the same ideal destination, which has been defined by actors in the Global North.

In response to critiques of the inaccurate geographic binary embedded in the concepts, I instead interpret *Global North* and *Global South* in non-literal terms, as Dados and Connell (2012) describe, as a metaphor or "an allegorical application of categories to name patterns of wealth, privilege, and development across broad regions," which includes "an entire history of colonialism, neo-imperialism, and differential economic and social change through which large inequalities in living standards, life expectancy, and access to resources are maintained" (p. 14). As Mahler (2018) describes, "the Global South does not refer simplistically to the geography of the Southern Hemisphere, but rather to a geographically flexible, sociospatial mapping of the negative effects of capitalist accumulation" (p. 3). Therefore, in contrast to the literal geographic interpretation, I view Global North/Global South as more of a political economy concept, and as applied in this book, a vehicle to explore the "dynamics of global power structures and dominant social groups across spatial scales" (Clarke, 2018). In this way, the distinction offers some fluidity, so countries, groups, and communities are not fixed as either in the North or South.

Moreover, when relaying the qualitative findings herein, from a more practical standpoint, the majority of my interview respondents readily employed the Global North/Global South distinction, and so my use allows some terminological consistency. Similarly, in the network analysis, organizations were coded based on headquarter country income level, where northern organizations are located in a high- or upper–middle-income country, and southern organizations are located in a lower- or lower–middle-income country. In some cases, I do use the term *developing country*, but this primarily refers to a label given by the organizations analyzed (e.g., the "Developing Country Partners" of GPE). I also often describe the arena in which educational aid actors work as *international development*, which, while acknowledging critiques of the developed/developing concept, again reflects a term commonly invoked by respondents and, moreover, that I employ to define an industry, not nations or peoples.

RATIONALE FOR THIS BOOK

I have researched international aid to education for over a decade, including analyses of several global governance organizations, their policies on aid, policymaking processes, and the outcomes of such processes. In each study, regardless of my methodological approach, or even the research questions I posed, four recurrent themes emerged. First, the aid-to-education environment has changed rather dramatically over recent years and continues to evolve at a rapid pace. This new aid arena is increasingly complex and currently includes greater numbers of more diverse actors than ever before. Second, and relatedly, the private sector, in particular corporate actors affiliated with businesses and philanthropies, is increasingly visible in global education advocacy and decisionmaking spaces, and an assumed contributor to policy-related discussions on education in the Global South. These two trends connect to a third, overarching theme emerging from my past work: an increase in rhetoric about partnership and the growth of partnership-based organizations and initiatives in education and international development. Finally, in each study that I have conducted on global education and aid, the issue of North/South power dynamics has arisen, even in cases where I was not investigating power or influence. In interviews especially, in relaying opinions and anecdotes, respondents described the roles of actors from the Global North and South as readily falling into long-established and expected hierarchical positions, with those from the North clearly retaining power. Respondents' descriptions of power dynamics consistently presented stark contrasts to my understanding of rhetoric from organizations in their documents and media. This book aims to braid these interrelated themes and explore the current state of partnership-based environments, including how we got here and possible paths forward.

Understanding power dynamics in this era of partnership holds relevance for two overarching reasons. The first is instrumental, relating to the effectiveness of development and humanitarian policies and programs. Research has shown that a lack of local participation results in poorer outcomes, where consistent input from recipients of aid, at all stages ranging from policymaking to implementation, is necessary for contextualized (and thereby effective) aid programs. Another instrumental rationale for this book relates to questions concerning the private sector in the educational arena and whether unelected business-oriented actors, often untrained in the areas of education and international development, are truly meeting aspirations and providing what is needed for more effective aid.

A second reason for investigating these intersecting themes is normative in nature; it asks whether the current aid environment can be considered just. Despite best efforts and institutional rhetoric against unequal degrees of influence and participation, an aid arena that subjugates southern voices and perpetuates the dominance of actors from the Global North must be critiqued on ethical grounds. An aid environment that retains northern organizations that give aid in positions of power arguably reinscribes colonial practices. What is more, to elevate unelected private actors to positions of policymakers through an aspirational discourse based primarily on their fiscal clout acts to preserve an already stark divide between those who have resources and those who do not, exacerbating already-troubling inequities.

Ramalingam (2013, pp. 88–89) clearly captures this ethical position on equity and participation in aid:

> The moral case for better engagement, ownership, and so on, is clear and well established. Calls have been made for a greater focus on developing country actors since the very start of the aid effort. And yet, if you ask anyone in any part of the aid sector today "Who calls the shots?," you are likely to be directed to an actor higher up in the "aid chain." Southern non-governmental organizations are controlled by Northern ones, non-governmental organizations, by UN agencies, both of these latter by donors, donors by political powers,

political powers by immediate electoral demands and more shadowy "strategic interests". . . . This clearly conflicts with the stated moral position of aid agencies of existing to help others. One of the ways this is maintained is through an almost legitimized lack of sensitivity to context, which allows a narrow, self-interested morality to prevail . . . aid agencies pay less attention to context than did their colonial forerunners—is sadly hard to deny.

Recipients of aid should be placed at the center of decisionmaking on policies and processes that directly affect them, not simply because contextualized development practices are more effective, but because to exclude southern actors, or to only allow symbolic or surface-level participation, amounts to paternalistic echoes of colonial practices.

Motivated by these rationales, the overarching aim of this book is to question the unproblematized embracing of partnership in global education policy through analytically uncovering power dynamics and hierarchies within partnership structures. In this book, I expose some fundamental flaws in what has come to be a prevalent trend in international development practice. With a growing number of partnerships aiming to reconstitute the international aid architecture by shifting power dynamics, this text exposes the ways in which partnerships have instead preserved the hierarchies they seek to eliminate. Beyond offering critiques, I also take the position that these inequities need not be inevitable, and present ways that the international aid community might reconceptualize partnerships.

A NOTE ON SCOPE

This book, I acknowledge, has a limited scope. I focus nearly exclusively on global-level partnerships and the strata of global governance. However, partnerships as a trend, their growth, the inclusion of the private sector, and issues relating to North/South power dynamics, are equally as prevalent and significant at country levels. A broader vertical analysis (see Vavrus & Bartlett, 2009) likely would have captured some of these dynamics at multiple levels, but unfortunately that was beyond the scope and focus of my research. Moreover, even at the global level, my in-depth qualitative work focuses on MSPs that apply vertical pooled funding mechanisms to support education. Many different types of partnerships, several of which I describe in Chapter 2, are also worthy of study, and perhaps case studies of different types of partnerships might counter some of my findings.

This book offers evidence based on a wide range of data collected over a span of several years. I made every effort to update and confirm that my findings remain relevant through follow-up interviews and analyses of more recent documents, but of course, I acknowledge the possibility that parts of my analysis may apply to less recent sources.

Also related to timing, much as some of the interview respondents mentioned, each of the case studies, as well as the organizations included in the network mapping, can be considered moving targets. As relatively new organizations, MSPs are constantly evolving, adopting new policies, mandates, and processes, as well as new partners. In this way, my conclusions apply to a particular point in time, and there is a strong likelihood that both GPE and ECW will have changed in many ways by the time these words are read.

As stated previously, my analyses of GPE and ECW are based on two sources of data: key informant interviews and publicly available documents and media. I acknowledge that direct observations of meetings and other internal institutional activities may have offered some insights that contrast with my findings. However, my interviews with key informants elicited deep and thoughtful responses from actors directly engaged with the organizations' design, governance, and activities. In presenting evidence in this book, I make clear that my findings were corroborated through directly quoting several responses, and I believe that my assurances of anonymity allowed a majority of key informants to speak freely and in a forthcoming manner.

A final note (which might be interpreted as a limitation by some) relates to the critical standpoint I adopt throughout this book. I wish to make clear that I believe partnership organizations have the potential to spur positive and crucial changes in global education, and they rest on foundational principles with which I agree. Moreover, the individuals who work within these organizations and their partners are not the objects of my criticism. Instead, I aim to expose power dynamics that reflect wider, structural issues that appear to arise regardless of individual actor intentions and despite the very genuine best of intentions.

MY POSITION AS AUTHOR

Throughout the writing of this book, and while conducting the research that has informed it, I have continually reflected upon my own positionality. This book directly addresses issues of power, in particular as relating to the dominant roles of actors from the Global North. And so I feel it imperative to acknowledge that the findings I convey throughout this book result from studies funded by northern-based agencies. I, moreover, situate myself as a researcher and writer from and based in the Global North, privileged to have been born and educated in Canada. My privilege also derives from the language that I speak, my economic class, and my professional status. Yet, at the same time, as the child of an immigrant from India, I also consider myself to hold a particular degree of embodied understanding and awareness of the experiences and positionality of those from the Global South, allowing me to approach my research on power dynamics and North/South hierarchies in a deeper and more nuanced way. Finally, I approach this work not from the position of an expert, wielding more knowledge than others, but instead as one who is in a privileged position to deliver evidence that I hope will contribute to a dialogue on addressing the power asymmetries that I identify.

OVERVIEW OF THE BOOK

This book is divided into six chapters. This introduction has sought to explain some of my interpretations of terms and concepts, detailing as well my conceptual framework, methodological choices, and scope. The rest of the book consists of five additional chapters.

Chapter 2 provides a historical and contemporary overview to help situate the book in past and current events, and it explains what is meant by an "era" of partnership. The chapter traces partnership-based mandates from the early establishment of the Bretton Woods organizations, through the end of the Cold War, when the era of partnership in development truly took hold. I explain how partnership as an ideal responded to critiques of the World Bank-led structural adjustment programs (SAPs) and the loss of Cold War rationales for aid policies. I give an overview of the partnership era's early days in the 1990s when a series of global mandates embraced the ideal and new forms of organizations based on partnership principles were established (namely, MSPs). I explain that notions of partnership are often conflated with PPPs and describe what qualifies as the private sector, as well as the roles that private actors play in global education policy. I also introduce here the concept of *private authority,* which applies, as shown in later chapters, to analyses of MSPs. The chapter offers a review of several critiques of partnerships, primarily from academic literature, but also from development practitioners, including issues of effectiveness and governance inefficiencies in MSPs and the ambiguity of partnership-based concepts and mandates. Because of my focus in this book, I pay particular attention here to critiques relating to power hierarchies and inequities within partnerships, as well as the role of private actors within partnerships. Chapter 2 closes with brief descriptions of several partnership-based organizations in education.

In Chapter 3, I argue for a network conceptualization of the actors, organizations, and relationships embedded in the aid-to-education arena and show how a network approach allows an empirical, quantitative analysis of power not only within a partnership, but across different partnerships. The chapter offers an exploration of the changing nature of the aid architecture, detailing how various researchers have conceptualized a new and evolving environment. I also explore the nature of power, offering particular conceptualizations specific to network analysis, defining how power dynamics might be observed within a network. I posit that networks hold the potential to reproduce power hierarchies, countering claims made by some scholars who argue that a networked environment is equitable. I support my claim through examples of various studies on international development and aid that apply network analysis to understand power, including a study that specifically analyzes educational partnerships. This research explores, via a cross-organizational network analysis, the current era of partnership through analyzing the interconnections between several transnational partnership-based organizations, such as the UNGEI, the INEE, the GPE, the Global Campaign for Education (GCE), and the GBC-E. This analysis of an original data set exposes power hierarchies within and across organizations, suggesting that the shift toward partnership perpetuates rather than transforms power relationships in international development education. In particular, donors maintain a position within the network that suggests that they wield the greatest influence over both the resource flows and normative preferences of partnerships.

Chapter 4 provides a qualitative study of the largest and most prominent MSP in the education sector. In this chapter, I detail a history of GPE and current power hierarchies, in particular the influence carried by donors, the World Bank, issues relating to language, and logistical constraints on participation. After describing some explicit efforts toward true partnership, I explain that structural power arguably makes such power hierarchies inevitable. This chapter also examines private actors' engagement in GPE, how their participation in the partnership came about, and their roles and degrees of influence. From presenting findings on private-sector engagement, I move to analyzing the complex nature of private authority within GPE. This chapter shows that in spite of efforts to create a more equitable environment via the GPE, actors from the Global North—particularly donors, the World Bank, and private actors—occupy higher hierarchical positions through the maintenance of structures that reproduce their dominant statuses, and through discourse that perpetuates the value of private authority, thereby countering the very goals that underpin the GPE's mandate.

Chapter 5 examines power dynamics within ECW, a global fund to support education in contexts of conflict, crisis, and fragility. After reviewing the relatively recent history and mandate of the partnership, I examine power dynamics through the lens of its governance, including the representation of certain actors, the dominance of UNICEF, and issues of coordination and competition within the education and humanitarianism sectors. The chapter then reviews dynamics at the country level, including limited community and local government participation. This case also examines the growing roles played by private actors, in particular the members of the GBC-E, and their discursive framing in ECW rhetoric relative to their actual roles within the partnership. I present private participation in ECW as an example of private authority, based on particular discourse surrounding the assumed value of private participation.

The book concludes with Chapter 6, in which I provide a summative exploration of my findings, bridging the network analysis with the case studies of GPE and ECW. In this final chapter, I revisit the conceptual framework detailed in this introduction, and in particular discuss the various ways in which structural and productive power have come to light through the research I present throughout this book. The conclusion reiterates the argument that key power imbalances persist in international aid to education, throwing faith in partnership into question. I discuss the broad implications of these findings and possible paths forward, including describing some possible characteristics of an aid-to-education environment that reflects equitable and genuine partnership.

NOTES

1. For examples of participation typologies, see Arnstein (1969), Pretty (1995), and White (1996).

2. Independent respondents include those who have engaged with MSPs but are not currently employed by an MSP, partner organization, or government, including academics, researchers, advisors, consultants, and others who now work outside of the development or humanitarian sectors.

3. The roles of respondents in interview citations are termed slightly differently in the GPE and ECW cases, based largely on how groups of stakeholders are labeled in rhetoric from each partnership (e.g., civil society versus NGOs). GPE board constituencies include only two representatives, so when discussing GPE board-level dynamics, I chose to code very generally based on broad constituency categories—otherwise, the person speaking would likely be very easy to identify.

CHAPTER 2

The Shift to Partnership in International Development and Education

My focus on partnerships in educational development, aid, and global governance stems from a recent discursive shift. Partnership as a concept has increasingly dominated the lexicon of international organizations, described by some as ubiquitous. Although partnership has long been put forward as a means to improve development practice, the idea truly took hold in the late 1990s. By the mid-2000s, forming and strengthening partnerships became standard and expected rhetoric within aid policies (Abrahamsen, 2004; Barnes & Brown, 2011; Crawford, 2003). As this chapter will detail, the partnership ideal has pervaded all sectors of development, and education is no exception. As Klees and Qargha (2014) describe of the education and development arena: "This is a world of partnership—with a vengeance. Everyone says they are partners with everyone else" (p. 327).

Although first coming to discursive prominence decades ago, partnership remains one of the most dominant objectives of development policies. For instance, the recently established Sustainable Development Goals (SDGs) are underpinned by the concept, which is solidified in SDG number 17, "Partnerships for the Goals": "The SDGs can be realized only with a strong commitment to global partnership and cooperation" (UNDP, 2018). As Adams and Judd (2018) describe, a "promotion of the partnership approach has accelerated since 2015" (p. 3). As this chapter later discusses, the growing number of roles for private-sector actors is inextricably tied to the partnership trend, given that the international community—including within the SDGs—frequently conflates the term *partnership* with *public–private partnership (PPP)*.

The widely embraced concept of partnership stands as relatively unproblematized. This chapter aims to uncover how we arrived at this era of partnership, which ideas and events drove a widespread acceptance of partnership as a development goal, what these historical foundations mean for current partnerships in development, the roles and new authority of private actors within these partnerships, and critiques of partnership rhetoric and practice. I provide an overview of several partnerships specific to the education sector, paying particular attention to the Education Cannot Wait Fund (ECW) and Global Partnership for Education (GPE)—the two multistakeholder partnerships (MSPs) on which I focus in this book.

THE ERA OF PARTNERSHIP

At its foundation, the notion of partnership relates strongly to the idea of cooperation. International cooperation most clearly began in earnest after World War II, with the establishment of the Bretton Woods organizations in 1944, eventually becoming the modern-day World Bank and International Monetary Fund (IMF), as well as the establishment of the United Nations in 1945. Through partnerships of donors, these new multilateral agencies sought to reconstruct a devastated postwar Europe. Prior to the mid-1940s, governments provided aid free from any coordination with others, but a new era of international cooperation was driven by a partnership ideal that remains familiar today: the optimistic notion that working together in cooperation and collaboration would lead to more effective and efficient delivery of development assistance (Riddell, 2007).

During the Cold War period, motivations for development aid were relatively clear. Although a degree of altruism certainly underpinned rich countries' participation in development, capitalist governments largely saw aid as a way to elicit the support of postcolonial countries while also promoting democracy and capitalism—essentially buying allies. Donors gained strategic advantages economically, militarily, and politically from giving aid. In theory, by adopting market-based growth strategies promoted by high-income capitalist donors, recipient nations would refrain from adopting communist ideals. The Cold War thereby gave a stable foundation to international aid policies, predominantly driven by a common goal to retain alliances, and for some, to solidify global capitalism (Barnes & Brown, 2011; Crawford, 2003; Riddell, 2007).

Yet with the end of the Cold War, development aid faced a crisis of purpose. Capitalist countries no longer needed to build strategic advantage via aid-based alliances. Moreover, a group of socialist donors no longer existed. In response, bilateral governments and multilaterals failed to provide clear or convincing rationales for giving international aid (Barnes & Brown, 2011; Crawford, 2003; Fowler, 2000; Riddell, 2007).

At the same time, the market-based ideologies that had driven many aid policies throughout the 1980s were increasingly called into question, in terms of both their efficacy and ethical implications. In particular, structural adjustment programs (SAPs) imposed complex conditions on recipient countries, requiring the adoption of policies underpinned by neoliberal principles, such as the opening of free markets and trade, increased privatization of traditionally public services—including education—and general reduction in state expenditures. By the end of the 1980s, over 100 countries were subject to SAPs, reflecting uniformity in development ideas and policies. Yet while these market-driven reforms were steadfastly promoted by such agencies as the World Bank, IMF, and several donors, after over a decade of SAPs, grave criticisms of these aid conditionalities were beginning to take hold. By the mid-1990s, SAPs were widely considered ineffective; they had not spurred substantial economic growth in recipient countries and had severe impacts on social services. Critics viewed this era of aid as exacerbating social inequities, exemplifying problematic paternalistic development ideologies (Barnes & Brown, 2011; Fowler, 2000; Klees, 2008b; Riddell, 2007).

The structural adjustment period deeply affected education sectors throughout the Global South. SAPs endorsed such prescriptions as increased private-sector involvement in educational provision, school fees, decentralization of school management, and reallocation of funds from higher to primary education due to the assumed contribution to human capital that would result. The educational mandate that promoted these market-oriented policies was termed by Colclough as the "Edlib" agenda due to its adherence to neoliberal principles, yet the policies were nonetheless widely supported as conditional for the receipt of development aid (Colclough, 2000). In the SAP/Edlib period, clear compulsory power was at work, where international financial institutions enforced the adoption of stipulated policies in exchange for assistance, leaving recipient countries with few options. Critiques of the education policies themselves, as well as widespread questioning of the broader conditional nature of lending, led to extensive disenchantment and skepticism of international organizations, most notably the World Bank and IMF (Jones, 2007; Klees, Samoff, & Stromquist, 2012; Mundy & Verger, 2015; Riddell, 2007).

These critiques, largely levied by civil society organizations (CSOs) and academic researchers, fed public perceptions in the 1990s that aid simply did not work, and indeed did much harm, leading to tempered public support and reduced aid budgets overall. This pessimistic mood, in conjunction with the vacuum in purpose left by the end of the Cold War and rising criticism of the ethical impacts of market-based development policies, left the aid world in a crisis state in search of a remedy. A new framing of international aid was desperately needed that would provide a clear purpose and lend new legitimacy to aid actors, institutions, and policies. In 1994, the need for this new framing was discussed at an Organisation of Economic Co-operation and Development, Development Assistance Committee (OECD DAC) meeting, where representatives sought to establish a new narrative that would convey a common development goal that everyone—governments, aid actors, and the public alike—could get behind. Partnership became the new narrative (Abrahamsen, 2004; Barnes & Brown, 2011; Fowler, 2000; Riddell, 2014).

Partnerships discourse

In 1996, the OECD DAC released the report *Shaping the 21st century: The Contribution of Development Co-operation*, which conveyed an initial concept of and rationale for partnership:

> In a partnership, development co-operation does not try to do things for developing countries and their people, but with them. It must be seen as a collaborative effort to help them increase their capacities to do things for themselves (OECD, 1996, p. 13).

move towards locally driven ownership

Partnership was a central tenet of the report, which proposed that the international development community's "understanding of development and development co-operation has undergone fundamental change" (p. 13), stressing that "[e]ach donor's programmes and activities should then operate within the framework of that locally owned strategy in ways that respect and encourage strong local commitment, participation, capacity development and ownership" (p. 14). The report identified particular priorities, using carefully chosen rhetoric that would in turn lay the foundation for future aid discourse (Riddell, 2007). Prominent among these new objectives were country ownership of development processes and the associated need for donor and recipient governments to engage with each other as partners.

This partnership rhetoric served to counter the crisis that aid actors were witnessing, including low levels of public support and criticisms of recent aid policies. As Fowler (2000) summarizes:

> The purpose of the "partnership" framework is to address what recent diagnoses of the aid industry conclude are the critical gaps which accounted in the past for the ineffectiveness of aid. These are identified as: (1) the lack of local "ownership" of policies and programmes, perceived as the key to good management; (2) inappropriate donor behaviour, including [insufficient] aid co-ordination and the ineffectiveness of conditionality as a surveillance and quality control mechanism; and (3) the underlying environment, including the nature of policies, institutions and the political system. (p. 5)

The partnership mandate was chosen to support development agendas for a few key reasons. As I explain next, the concept of partnership is often critiqued as fuzzy or malleable. Yet the vague nature of the term, allowing many interpretations, in fact led to its adoption. The ambiguity of the partnership concept allowed members of competing ideological camps to embrace the idea as a way forward, concurrently placating critics who condemned aid policies' impacts on equity and social justice, as well as those who were concerned with ineffectiveness and corruption. A positive attribute of partnership as an ideal was its "normative malleability," and through its adoption, the OECD DAC created and convinced others that the partnership policy narrative could transform the aid regime, leading to widespread buy-in (Barnes & Brown, 2011, p. 172).

Most notably, the discourse of partnership suggested that power asymmetries between actors and organizations in the Global North and Global South would be reversed, with recipient countries now considered partners that not only participated in the design, but *owned* their development policies (Abrahamsen, 2004). As described in Chapter 1, partnership models are predicated upon ideals around participation and country ownership, and they "suggest a redistribution of power from the domestic and foreign stakeholders who normally formulate development policy in heavily indebted countries to marginalized communities traditionally excluded from the policy process" (Vavrus & Seghers, 2010, p. 78).

[margin note: Partnerships btw actors/ orgs in the Global North +South + recipient countries]

The concept of partnership was a goal toward which everyone could ascribe. Even the World Bank, the object of most criticism during the SAP era, identified partnership as a key guiding principle for its future policy work. In 1998, then-World Bank president James Wolfensohn put forth the idea of partnership, describing a true partnership as "led by governments and parliaments of the countries" where local actors are "in the driver's seat" (Wolfensohn, 1998, p. 7–9).

Since the late 1990s, the development community increasingly and enthusiastically adopted the narrative, culminating in the inclusion of a partnership-based goal in the Millennium Development Goals (MDG) as number 8, "To Develop a Global Partnership for Development." This goal, which promoted increased collaboration between UN agencies, governments, private-sector actors, and civil society, signified the narrative's infusion into the development lexicon (Barnes & Brown, 2011; Barnes, Brown, & Harman, 2016).

And partnership as a goal has since been enshrined in several global declarations. For instance, in 2002, a conference held in Monterrey, Mexico, and attended by lead government actors, nonstate representatives, and the heads of several international organizations, resulted in the Monterrey Consensus—a global response to the challenges of aid, listing commitments made to improve financing for international development (UN, 2003). Here, as stated by Robert Picciotto, the Director-General of Operations Evaluation at the World Bank: "Broad agreement was reached at Monterrey regarding the basic elements of a new *global partnership*," indicating a "new development paradigm" (2002, p. 3, emphasis in original). As the Monterrey Consensus states: "Effective partnerships among donors and recipients are based on the recognition of national leadership and ownership of development plans" (UN, 2003, p. 14). International agreement on the need to improve and revamp the aid agenda culminated in the Paris Declaration on Aid Effectiveness in 2005, which was widely endorsed by heads of multilateral and bilateral agencies alongside ministers of countries throughout the Global North and South. In it, "Ownership" is the first of five central principles, in which "partner countries exercise effective leadership over their development policies and strategies and co-ordinate development actions" and donors commit to "respect[ing] partner country leadership and help[ing] strengthen their capacity to exercise it" (OECD, 2005, p. 3). The rhetoric of the Paris Declaration reflected a need to reconceptualize relationships. Donors were urged to better align their processes with the local systems of countries receiving aid, which in the Declaration were depicted frequently as *partners*. The Paris Declaration was complemented by the 2008 Accra Agenda for Action and the 2011 Busan Partnership for Effective Development Co-Operation documents, which set out to operationalize its principles (OECD, 2008, 2011).

In education, the 1990 World Congress on Education for All (EFA) reflected the emergent partnership trend, as one of the early collaborative efforts to support universal access to education. EFA signified a new consensus around global education norms, widely viewed as a global compact on education. This compact also underpinned the second MDG of achieving universal primary education, which was supported by a wide range of international agencies and nongovernmental organizations (NGOs) (Chabbott, 2003; Mundy, 2012).

Although I argue throughout this book that partnerships tend to reflect structural and productive power, the EFA movement in fact provides an exemplar of the exercise of institutional power. EFA began as a global movement to promote universal education, spurred by a series of conferences, attended by representatives from multilateral agencies, governments, and civil society, that established firm mandates and frameworks for nations to follow in an effort to provide schooling to all, such as gender-equity measures and early childhood programs (UNESCO, 2000). Yet although EFA was touted as the result of widespread consensus, critics argued that countries were compelled to agree to a particular agenda, driven by the norms and preferences of international organizations and professionals, which suggested a form of indirect coercion (Chabbott, 2003). Within the EFA movement, institutional power indirectly compelled actors to adopt its agenda (Brock-Utne, 2001; Mundy, 2012). In the subsequent years, organizations promoted EFA while simultaneously adopting partnership-related goals.

Although both institutional and compulsory power were certainly exercised beyond the 1990s, I argue that structural and productive power became increasingly dominant as the partnership narrative grew more prevalent. The partnership era we see today, in fact, reflects a movement away from compulsory power specifically. A belief in partnership as a conduit for more effective, equitable aid has led to the establishment of several new collaborative educational funding agencies, many of which explicitly ground their guiding principles in the Paris Declaration. Yet power asymmetries remain, even within newly formed organizations that explicitly shun coercive aid practices.

MULTISTAKEHOLDER PARTNERSHIPS

The shift to partnership in international development manifested in several ways and engendered common aid policies and global governance practices. First, as described previously, global agreements on development and aid, including the Paris Declaration, included the goal of partnership as a core element. Second, partnership rose to prominence in the internal policies and mandates of international aid organizations, with the OECD, World Bank, European Union, and others all adopting it as part of their strategic plans.

Third, new collaborative transnational organizations were established, underpinned by partnership ideals, and given various labels, such as *global partnerships, global funds,* or *transnational PPPs.* I focus on such organ- izations in this book and have chosen to use the term *multistakeholder part-nerships (MSPs)* to refer to them. [*terminology*]

MSPs are organizational manifestations of the Paris principles. They have proliferated in recent years, initiated to tackle single issue areas, such as communicable disease, water, the environment, and education. MSPs are sometimes described as *vertical funds* because they provide funding to a single sector, in contrast to *horizontal funds,* which target a range of sectors. As [*key & learning*] partnership organizations, MSPs bring together stakeholders from the state and nonstate sectors—hence the public–private element—and from the Global North and South into single decisionmaking forums to collaborate and coordinate policies on development funding (Bäckstrand, 2008; Lele, Sadik, & Simmons, 2007; Savedoff, 2012; Severino & Ray, 2010). Widely touted as responses to the principles set out in the Paris Declaration, MSPs promote coordination, country ownership, and, of course, partnership (Bezanson & Isenman, 2012; Savedoff, 2012; Severino & Ray, 2010). More recently, MSPs have been considered a key element to the success of the SDGs, which can [*power to mobilize &*] be "complemented by multi-stakeholder partnerships that mobilize and share knowledge, expertise, technology and financial resources, to support the achievement of the sustainable development goals in all countries, in particular developing countries" (UN, 2016).

Although each is structured differently, common characteristics of MSPs include constituency-based governance arrangements designed in an effort to include an array of voices in decisionmaking. MSP governance boards generally include governments, multilaterals, civil society, companies, and foundations. Whereas traditional aid was dominated by bilateral funding to a single country, MSPs act as collaborative spaces where aid can be harmonized and coordinated into single, pooled funds. Finally, the ideal of country ownership lies at the core of MSP mandates and processes, as stressed in the Paris Declaration principles, where recipient countries are viewed as partners with equal input into the policies and operations of the organization (Bezanson & Isenman, 2012; Buse & Tanaka, 2011; Lele et al., 2007).

The health sector includes some of the most prominent MSPs, including the Global Fund to Fight AIDS, Tuberculosis, and Malaria, GAVI: The Vaccine Alliance, the Global Alliance for Improved Nutrition (GAIN), the International Health Partnership, and the Roll Back Malaria Partnership (Bezanson & Isenman, 2012; Frenk & Suerie, 2013). Other social sectors have been the focus of MSPs, including the Global Water Partnership, the Consultative Group of the Cities Alliance, and the Consultative Group to Assist the Poor (Bezanson & Isenman, 2012). As described later in this chapter, several partnership-based organizations have been established in the area of education. Two of the most prominent of these MSPs are the GPE and the ECW—the two cases I explore in most depth throughout this book.

MSPs result from a major shift in international relations, where the dominant state-centric model of the past three centuries gave way to an ostensibly nonhierarchical form of governance. Emerging against the backdrop of globalization is what Ruggie (2004) describes as "a fundamental reconstitution of the global public domain: away from one that equated the 'public' in international politics with states and the interstate realm, to one in which the very system of states is becoming embedded in a broader, albeit still thin and partial, institutionalized arena" (p. 2). This global public domain has necessitated global public policies to ensure the provision and financing of collective goods that affect cross-border populations (Kaul, Conceicao, Le Goulven, & Mendoza, 2003; Stone, 2008). In the absence of a world government, other bodies have emerged to design global public policies relating to a variety of social sectors. Although many international organizations still include solely high-income–government representatives, MSPs have elevated the nonstate sector and actors from the Global South to roles in nonhierarchical decisionmaking on global policies.

Arguably, any form of global governance embodies a deficit of democratic legitimacy, where decisions are made "at best—on very limited explicit consent from the affected populations" (Scholte, 2002, p. 289). By embracing a variety of representatives from different sectors and geographical scope into collaborative policymaking, MSPs attempt to counter this lack of wider public participation, enabling a "space of assembly" where diverse constituencies can participate in policy design (Stone, 2008, p. 23). MSPs moreover reflect changes in the structure of development financing with pooled, vertical funding, into which all donors merge resources for disbursement to a single sector. Therefore, MSPs reflect a shift in both the "how" (vertical funding and constituency-based collaborative policymaking) and the "who" (representatives from the nonstate sector and the Global South) of development aid.

Although the partnership trend has manifested in several ways, I choose to focus on MSPs in this book due to the extent to which they clearly signify the partnership narrative in organizational form. MSP mandates and objectives, as well as their inclusion of particular stakeholders, reflect the core elements of partnership as advocated by the Paris Declaration and other global mandates. MSPs overwhelmingly claim to embrace and promote country ownership and the participation of southern beneficiaries in decision-making. Their inclusion of the private sector is particularly notable, given the growing roles of businesses and foundations in development. MSPs are also relatively new organizations (most of them were established in the past decade or so). They are growing in number, disburse increasing sums of aid dollars, and are understudied. And the value and impact of MSPs remain an open question.

PARTNERSHIPS AS PUBLIC-PRIVATE ARRANGEMENTS

As previously stated, organizations and actors in international development frequently conflate *partnerships* with *PPPs*. In fact, a common alternative term for MSPs is *transnational PPPs*, given the joining of state and nonstate actors. The key nonstate actors considered the core players in many partnerships are private-sector companies or foundations. In describing the partnership model of development, Adams and Judd (2018) explain that private actors play a key role: "Inadequate financing of the UN and its mandates has also prompted the UN and its Member States to embrace a range of different private sector partnerships and finance patterns, including through philanthropies and big business . . . at the global level these have taken the form of multi-donor or multi-stakeholder partnerships to achieve specific goals" (p. 3).

Understanding PPPs depends largely on knowing what exactly constitutes the "private" element. Because education is a key contributor to what is commonly viewed as the "public good," policymakers and practitioners often presume that systems of education and those involved in education are fundamentally public (Menashy, 2009). However, private actors—including families, students, communities, charities, and businesses—have long had significant input into schools and broader education systems, contributing to educational policy and practice in a range of ways. While most definitions of the private sector include some allusion to being apart from government, or "nonstate," precisely defining private participation in education presents a challenging task because the private sector is vast, essentially encompassing any actor or entity apart from the state.

While acknowledging the sector's breadth, my concern herein involves an admittedly narrow definition of *private sector* as it is more commonly applied in the context of education and development—namely, actors affiliated with businesses, which include both companies and corporate foundations. The private sector, broadly understood, unquestionably occupies an increasingly prominent role in the global education arena. Yet in rhetoric on PPPs, and as related to global partnerships, business-affiliated actors most often align with the term *private* (Robertson, Mundy, Verger, & Menashy, 2012).

Businesses that engage in international development activities and participate in global partnerships do so as part of a larger business objective, often as part of their corporate social responsibility (CSR) programs. CSR activities are integral to a company's profit-oriented goals and are often funded through its general operating budget. CSR programs promote a variety of activities, including cash contributions made to support a specific cause; in-kind contributions, including such items as school supplies or classroom technology; and more leadership-oriented policy engagement, including participation in educational forums and playing advocacy roles concerning a particular issue (Bhanji, 2008; Menashy, 2013; van Fleet, 2012). As argued by Utting and Zammit (2009), corporations that promote their international work under the banner of CSR do so when "management recognizes that it is in the interests of a company to ratchet up its approach, moving from the initial phases centred on denial and public relations towards new business models characterized by proactivity and heightened responsiveness to both threats and opportunities," and arguably, the inclusion of corporations within partnerships is a "manifestation" of such processes (p. 43).

Foundations or philanthropies are often formed using the profits of corporate endeavors, but ostensibly they operate independent of business interests, and so they consider themselves separate from their associated corporation, where often the only overlap can be seen in name or sharing of leadership (Bhanji, 2008; Menashy, 2013). Some foundations function as grant-making bodies, while others finance their own programmatic activities. Most foundation funding directed toward education is spent in the United States, where philanthropists are seen as increasingly influential in public policymaking (Bhanji, 2012; Reckhow, 2013). But in the Global South, foundations are gaining prominence and are now members of several education-related partnerships (Srivastava, 2016; Srivastava & Oh, 2010).

It is important not to conflate foundations and companies. In the case study of GPE in Chapter 4, for instance, these two groups of private actors often conflict in terms of mandate and operations. Yet, in my view, both represent a particular shift in global governance, where actors affiliated with private companies—be they nonprofit or profit oriented—have increasingly been invited to participate as partners. This welcoming of the private sector is indicative of a new sense of urgency around the need for funding and expertise that foundations and companies can provide. Through both philanthropic endeavors and CSR programs, foundations and corporations have been financing, designing, and implementing education programs on a global scale. Companies and foundations now collaborate in education policymaking alongside both state and other nonstate actors within new partnerships. Although some partnerships are not inclusive of private actors, the majority have welcomed, and as will be argued, solicited increased private-sector participation.

As this book details, particularly in the case studies of GPE and ECW, many partnerships have been established in part to provide a space for

PRIVATE AUTHORITY ← new concept.

concern w private actors

increased public–private collaboration. My primary concern with regard to private actors in the context of partnerships relates to their roles as policy-makers that have been afforded legitimacy due to a particular discourse, holding literal seats at the table alongside public-sector and civil society partners.

As Utting and Zammit (2009) describe, "PPPs are also seen as a logical response to structural changes in state–market–society relations that have occurred since the 1980s. Globalisation, liberalization . . . have resulted in the rolling back of certain state functions and capacities, the massive growth in the number and global reach of corporations, and the emergence of new policy actors" (p. 43). The inclusion of the private sector in public policy decisionmaking via partnerships, therefore, reflects a convergence of recent trends, with the consequence of private actors embodying what international relations scholars have described as private authority in the global arena (Bhanji, 2012; Hall & Biersteker, 2002). Until recently, analysts of international relations have limited their foci to the actions of individual nations, assuming that nations are the only legitimate form of authority in the global sphere. However, in the context of new and globalized transnational arrangements, the private sector is not only widely considered to be a prominent player, but also one that embodies a new form of authority. As described by Hall and Biersteker (2002):

who are these new actors?

> While these new actors are not states, are not state-based, and do not rely exclusively on the actions or explicit support of states in the international arena, they often convey and/or appear to have been accorded some form of legitimate authority. That is, they perform the role of authorship over some important issue or domain. They claim to be, perform as, and are recognized as legitimate by some larger public (that often includes states themselves) as authors of policies, of practices, of rules, and of norms. . . . What is most significant, however, is that they appear to have been accorded a form of legitimate authority. (p. 4)

Two concepts help to define private authority: authority and legitimacy. *Authority* can be understood as when one actor or actors have an ability to "get other actors to defer judgement to them" and "requires some level of consent from other actors" (Barnett & Finnemore, 2005, pp. 169–170). This consent is often engendered through legitimacy. According to Keohane (2006), *legitimacy* has three main dimensions, which he classifies as normative, epistemic, and performative. These dimensions of legitimacy allow actors and organizations to achieve a particular appearance, as those who generate needed outputs and information and have the ability to solve problems. The interconnected concepts of authority and legitimacy, as well as the more specific concept of private authority, align closely with notions of power. Private authority relates to productive power because the discourse through which power works simultaneously allows particular actors to achieve authority and legitimacy. This affording of authority and legitimacy to the private sector will feature prominently in the two case studies presented later in this book.

Private-sector policy actors reflect a fairly recent shift in global governance, international development, and education, where those involved have traditionally occupied public-sector roles as elected government officials or state agents. But, as Bhanji (2012, p. 303) explains, we are witnessing "new forms of private authority—individuals or organizations that have decision-making power over a particular issue area and are regarded as exerting power legitimately. Private authority refers to situations where decision-making power and responsibility for public policy issues are no longer held solely by government." This concept of private authority holds much relevance when examining the roles of private actors during this era of partnership. The existence of MSPs indicates such a rise in private authority in global policymaking spaces, where nonstate actors are not merely a presence, but ostensibly legitimate *partners*.

Most MSPs include private partners in their governance structures, serving as board or steering committee members. Which types of companies are included, however, depends upon the issue that the PPP seeks to address. For example, GAVI: The Vaccine Alliance includes seats on its board of directors from the for-profit pharmaceutical industry, as well as a seat solely dedicated to the Bill and Melinda Gates Foundation (GAVI, 2018). GAIN includes on its board representatives from private banks, as well as private foundations, including the Children's Investment Fund Foundation and the Gates Foundation (GAIN, 2018). The Consultative Group of the Cities Alliance, which tackles urban poverty, includes only Omidyar Network as a private-sector partner (Cities Alliance, 2018).

In education, private-sector representatives occupy key policymaker roles in partnership governance, including several described later in this chapter. What is more, private actors have formed partnerships of their own, including the Global Business Coalition for Education (GBC-E) and the International Education Funders Group (IEFG).

Overall, as I argue throughout this book, private actors have emerged as core players in global education. Private authority reflects a complex interplay of actors and interests and relates to a dominant discourse that I argue supports the production of power within an already-unequal development aid architecture.

QUESTIONING PARTNERSHIPS

International development scholars have grappled with this surge in global partnerships. Some posit that partnerships are for the most part positive, most notably because they embrace southern participation and allow recipients of funding to have a voice in policy design, and thereby also promote contextualized implementation (Abrahamsen, 2004). But many researchers have questioned the shift toward partnership, drawing attention to both practical and ethical critiques.

Researchers have shown that MSPs in particular can be less than effective, especially in terms of governance and decisionmaking. MSPs have been plagued by unstable financing, vague accountability processes, and, as will be explored in the qualitative case studies of GPE and ECW later in this book, concerns regarding the growing dominance of the private sector (Bäckstrand, 2008; Buse & Tanaka, 2011; Global Fund, 2011; Lele et al., 2007; Martens, 2007).

A further critique has focused on the nature of constituency-based governance—a key feature of MSPs in which each group of stakeholders has board-level representation. This form of governance often results in tensions among board members and an associated inattention to critical policy-related discussions. For instance, in their survey review of global MSPs, Bezanson and Isenman of the Center for Global Development note that in an effort to be inclusive spaces, MSP boards are often inefficient, rarely engage in dialogue on substantive strategy questions, and sometimes enable conflicts of interest (Bezanson & Isenman, 2012). Similarly, an independent review of the Consultative Group for International Agricultural Research finds that its board reflects so many different perspectives and interests that decisionmaking becomes challenging (Bezanson, Narain, & Prante, 2004). A review of the Global Fund to Fight AIDS, Tuberculosis, and Malaria concludes that its board retreats to micromanagement rather than substantive agenda setting (Global Fund 2011), and a 2011 independent evaluation of those partnerships of which the World Bank is a member also critiques large, constituency-based boards as inefficient (IEG, 2011).

Furthermore, my past research on the GPE's governance reinforced these critiques (Menashy, 2017). I applied the divisive issue of private schooling as a lens to help in understanding policy-related decisionmaking among very different board members, and found that GPE had not substantively engaged with the issue of private education, which—to quote one of my interview respondents—reflected "strategic avoidance" due to concerns that a debate could destabilize the partnership. This absence of dialogue reflected broader GPE governance issues, where policy-related debates are rare. The coming together of such a range of organizational entities on the one hand arguably created a desirable diversity within a partnership, which responded to a need for inclusiveness and equal voice for all stakeholders. But on the other hand, the governance structure produced an environment where dialogue is challenging. Because this conclusion aligns with the evaluations of other similarly structured MSPs, together these studies call into question the effectiveness of the partnership-based model.

As previously mentioned, scholars have also critiqued the concept of partnership based on its very general definition, sometimes described as ambiguous and therefore difficult or even impossible to implement in practice. Although the intention of designers of partnership-based mandates such as the OECD DAC was to choose a narrative malleable enough to fit with any stakeholder vision, as a result, *partnership* is an excessively fuzzy term that could be adopted to fit any purpose. Partnerships are thereby viewed as simple rhetoric. In this way, the term could also be considered "misleading," and its use has arguably served to mute criticisms of development agencies that have not engaged in meaningful, equitable collaborative activities (Abrahamsen, 2004; Adams & Martens, 2016, p. 1; Klees, 2009; Samoff & Carrol, 2004).

Another critique questions the supposed value of collaborative, cooperative forums that are promoted within partnership organizations. As Fowler (2000) argues, assumptions embedded in partnership-based mandates imply that collaborative processes will necessarily lead to lasting change in international development policy, and conflict among actors is fundamentally problematic and ought to be avoided. However, "contention is needed just as often as cooperation, if those who are poor and marginalized are to have any hope of being heard and really listened to outside of aid inducement" (p. 5). Partnerships convey the assumption that working together in harmony will produce the best results, but this may not always be the case, as cooperative processes are more likely to benefit those traditionally in power rather than those who have been subjugated.

This issue of power underpins the questions that I pose throughout this book—specifically, whether power asymmetries exist, and whether partnerships potentially reinscribe hierarchies while simultaneously claiming to reduce inequities. Relating to issues of power within MSPs, the most dominant critique has addressed hierarchical relationships between the Global North and South, in spite of claims of equal partnership (Bezanson et al., 2004; Lele et al., 2007; Martens, 2007).

As Martens (2007) found in a study of health-focused partnerships:

> On paper many partnerships give the impression of equal rights for stakeholders and broad representation, but in practice it is the wealthy actors from the North who dominate, whether they are governments, corporations or private foundations. . . . With a few positive exceptions, multistakeholder partnerships reproduce precisely the power relationships and asymmetries that exist in the international system. In some senses they even intensify them by strengthening the dominance of a few powerful governments, multinationals, private foundations, and well organised international organisations from the North, while governments and civil society organisations from the South often play only a token role. (p. 41)

Critics have raised doubts concerning the supposed reversal of power arrangements that partnerships claim to support. On a practical level, creating "genuine" partnerships that shift power dynamics is viewed as an incredibly lofty endeavor, where even "commentators supportive of the general thrust of partnerships frequently draw attention to the difficulties in achieving 'genuine' partnership based on equality and mutual respect in a context where one party is in possession of the purse and the other the begging bowl" (Abrahamsen, 2004, p. 1454).

Given that traditional financing relationships remain intact, *[handwritten: Financing ↓ power]*

> The most frequently cited constraint to the formation of authentic partnerships is the control of money. Indeed it has been suggested that this may make true partnership impossible . . . this is a dialogue of the unequal, and however many claims are made for transparency or mutuality, the reality is—and is seen to be—that the donor can do to the recipient what the recipient cannot do to the donor. There is an asymmetry of power that no amount of well-intentioned dialogue can remove. (Lister, 2000, pp. 3–4) *[handwritten: ★ Last sentence ↑✓✗]*

On a deeper and more skeptical level, critics portray partnerships as masking the reinscription of donor dominance over recipient countries. The idea of partnership between actors from the Global North and Global South elicits skepticism, given that the partnership narrative originated in the Global North and supports northern agencies' need for greater legitimacy and public approval (Abrahamsen, 2004; Lister, 2000). As Crawford (2003) argues, "Contrary to the official discourse of partnership as encouraging locally formulated reform strategies, the notions of 'partnership' and 'local ownership' simultaneously disguise and legitimise the interventions of international agencies in domestic reform processes, serving to mystify power asymmetry" (p. 139). In this sense, although the rhetoric of partnership implies a change in development strategy away from conditionality-based aid, critics question whether relationships continue to operate with the exact power hierarchies of the past, but only under a different facade. *[handwritten: Mystify asymmetry]* Partnership-based initiatives, therefore, are deemed a mere disguise meant to allow donors the same degree of intervention into recipient country policies, but free from criticism because of donors' claims that they support country ownership. As Fowler (2000) puts it, "'partnership' is a terminological Trojan Horse" and

> is a more subtle form of external power imposition, less amenable to resistance. . . . By appearing to be benign, inclusive, open, all-embracing and harmonious, partnership intrinsically precludes other interpretations of reality, options and choices without overtly doing so. In sum, the selection and universal application of partnership is a mystification and distraction that not only conditions the

development debate at the cost of alternatives, but legitimizes deep penetration of foreign concerns into domestic processes, inviting perverse and negative reactions. (p. 7)

Scholars argue that partnerships lack self-evaluation and reflection and do little to interrogate power distribution among stakeholders (Morvaridi, 2012). This more subtle form of external power results from a shift from compulsory power, which was unequivocally observed during the era of strict conditionalities. Yet power now operates in a way that I argue reflects structural power. Throughout this book, I discuss the nature and provide evidence of the reproduction of structural power in educational partnerships, echoing many of these critiques.

Additionally, the concept of partnership has become synonymous with nonstate participation in development policy and practice, largely tantamount to PPPs. For example, with SDG number 17, "Partnerships for the Goals," targets include support to MSPs, which as I explain next include nonstate partners, and also to "encourage and promote public-private partnerships" (UNDP, 2018). As described at the Joint Thematic Forum on Partnerships at the United Nations in 2014:

> Member States should also introduce incentives for the private sector to contribute to development priorities. . . . Creating incentives to attract the private sector to partner with other actors will allow for governments to benefit from an increase of entrepreneurial enterprises in turn mobilizing more technology and resources to generate innovative solutions to critical development issues. Policymakers will need to think creatively about how to appropriately incentivize partnerships and ultimately investors to put money into sustainable development. (UN, 2014, pp. 5–6)

In education, a large body of literature has raised critiques of PPPs, in terms of global governance, public policy, and school provision. As will be thoroughly detailed in the qualitative case studies explored in Chapters 4 and 5, partnerships have elevated private actors—including representatives from companies and foundations—to influential public policymaking positions, eliciting critiques relating to private authority and democratic deficit in global governance. A related concept, philanthrocapitalism, also holds relevance for these cases. McGoey (2012) defines philanthrocapitalism as "the tendency for a new breed of donors to conflate business aims with charitable endeavors, making philanthropy more cost-effective, impact-oriented, and financially profitable" (p. 185). A key element of philanthrocapitalism is "the increased visibility of individual philanthropists as policy drivers," referring to the ways in which private actors have taken up positions of authority that allow them to steer policy dialogue and decisionmaking within public policy arenas (McGoey, 2012, p. 110). As I will discuss, a particular discourse relating to the assumed positive inputs of private actors drives an overwhelming embrace of and attempt to harness increased private-sector engagement within partnerships, reflecting productive power.

PARTNERSHIPS IN EDUCATION AND DEVELOPMENT

This book offers case studies of arguably the two most prominent education MSPs—the GPE and ECW—which will be described in more detail later. But several other partnership-based organizations and initiatives in the education sector have come to prominence, many of which were established only in the past few years. These partnerships might focus on funding; convene events; promote advocacy, knowledge mobilization, and mutual learning platforms; or offer policy guidance. Not all would be considered MSPs, nor do all combine public and private actors. But each has been designed in the spirit of partnership, and thus must be considered within the wider context of education and development, signifying both a practical and rhetorical shift toward more collaborative, partnership-based policy and practice arrangements. What is more, partnerships are interconnected via interlinking comemberships: many organizations are members of multiple partnerships. In this way, these partnerships create a network, which will be the subject of Chapter 3.

UNGEI, launched in 2000 by the United Nations during the World Education Forum in Dakar, is an MSP committed to increasing access to quality education for girls, and "contributing to the empowerment of girls and women through transformative education" (UNGEI, 2018). UNGEI serves as primarily an advocacy-oriented partnership and focuses largely on helping marginalized groups, eliminating gender-based violence in schools, and improving girls' learning and progress through secondary education (UNGEI, 2018).

The INEE, established in 2000, is an open, flexible, global multistakeholder network that includes a range of organizations and actors, including global and local NGOs, bilateral and multilateral aid agencies, research institutions, governments, schools, and populations affected by emergencies. The INEE facilitates (rather than operates) collaborative interagency relations to support work that focuses on education in contexts of conflict, fragility, and humanitarian crisis. INEE facilitates community building, and convenes events that bring together stakeholders "to foster dialogue, influence positive change in policy and practice, advance research to build the evidence, and support the establishment of partnerships to address common challenges and work towards shared solutions" (INEE, 2018). INEE also engages in knowledge management, advocacy campaigns, and research programs.

The IEFG, initiated in 2008, is an "affinity network" of foundations, donor-advised funds, corporate giving programs, and charities that finance education in low- and middle-income countries (IEFG, 2018). It now includes over 100 members and works to convene its membership to facilitate co-learning, networking, and information sharing on a wide range of issues and areas, primarily on basic education (IEFG, 2018).

The GBC-E was established in 2012 as a partnership-based convening body, which acts as an umbrella organization that unites and offers a voice for businesses involved in global education. Through coordinating, communicating, showcasing the value of business initiatives in education, and facilitating research into global education, the GBC-E allows "companies to become part of a global movement of businesses committed to changing children's lives through education" (GBC-E, 2016b). Although not a defined case study in this book, I will revisit the role of the GBC-E in future chapters, particularly Chapter 5, in which I discuss the role of the private sector in ECW.

The Africa and Middle East Education Outcomes Fund (EOF) was first announced in 2018 and will be launched as a pooled fund combining donor aid and philanthropic and corporate giving to partner with governments to support successful interventions in education. The EOF therefore aims to apply impact bonds at scale. Through this process, "EOF will ensure that funding only goes to what works and will systematically shift funds towards scaling programs that demonstrate the best results and value for money" (EOF, 2019; also see Brookings, 2018).

The Inclusive Education Initiative (IEI) was also announced in 2018 to coincide with the Global Disability Summit as a partnership between the UK Department for International Development (DfID) and the Norwegian Ministry of Foreign Affairs, and was hosted by the World Bank. This fund was designed in response to the need to target support toward the 65 million school-aged children with disabilities, nearly half of whom are out of school. The IEI also partners with UNICEF and GPE (World Bank, 2018b).

The International Financing Facility for Education (IFFEd) is another recently initiated (and yet to be launched) funding mechanism for education, where high-income, bilateral donors partner to provide guarantees that are then used to create new financing through enabling the major multilateral development banks—such as the World Bank Group, African Development Bank, Asian Development Bank, European Bank for Reconstruction and Development, and the Inter-American Development Bank—to target loans to lower–middle-income countries committed to investing in their education systems. For example, countries such as Vietnam, Kenya, Pakistan, and Guatemala have very large out-of-school populations, and yet they receive fewer international aid dollars than low-income countries and are ineligible for certain types of loans (Education Commission, 2019; Edwards, 2018a, 2018c; World Bank, 2018a).

Multistakeholder Case Studies: The Global Partnership for Education and the Education Cannot Wait Fund

In this book, I focus on two particular partnerships as case studies in order to offer deeper analyses of the ways that partnerships function, the challenges they face, and who wields power within them. These are the GPE and the ECW. As described previously, several partnerships have come to prominence in the education sector, but GPE and ECW present particularly interesting and important cases, with several common characteristics that together offer insights into new partnership-based organizations. As two of the largest global funds for education, established relatively recently and growing in size and reputation, both are PPPs, including northern government donors, recipient southern actors, multilateral agencies, civil society, private foundations, and companies, all acting as partners. Moreover, both include country ownership as an element to their mandates and strategic plans, with a stated importance of recipient voice and local participation. Next, I provide very brief descriptions of each, although more detail on GPE's and ECW's histories, mandates, and operations will be included in upcoming chapters.

GPE is an MSP dedicated to increasing access to quality education worldwide, supporting low-income countries that lack sufficient funds to provide quality basic education for all children (GPE, 2016a). Initially launched in 2002 by the World Bank, it was then called the EFA Fast Track Initiative (FTI), "a partnership between donor and developing countries to accelerate progress towards the Millennium Development Goal (MDG) of universal primary education" (World Bank, 2005, p. 2). However, the FTI came under scrutiny in the late 2000s, leading to a major restructuring and rebranding into the current GPE. GPE came to be governed by a constituency-based board of directors consisting of 19 voting members representing donor countries, recipient countries, multilateral agencies, CSOs, the private sector, and foundations. It includes over 70 developing country partners (DCPs) that receive resources via the GPE Fund, a pooled fund from which disbursements are made and that is financed predominantly by high-income, northern donor country partners. The World Bank acts as the GPE host, and the GPE offices are situated within the Bank's headquarters in Washington, DC (GPE, 2016b, 2016c, 2018b).

This book examines GPE as an exemplar for the recent trend of partnership, "underpinned by the principles set out in the March 2005 Paris Declaration on Aid Effectiveness" (GPE, 2012, p. 3). The organization's governance structure, in which all members are rhetorically defined as equal partners, particularly reflects the Paris principles. Its financing arrangements and decisionmaking processes, inclusive of local actors within recipient countries and based on country-owned policies, also signify the goal of partnership. The organization is committed to supporting "developing country partner governments to plan effectively for results, take the lead on delivery" (GPE, 2016c). The first "guiding principle" listed in its charter is "country ownership" (GPE, 2013a, p. 3). Its strategic plan similarly states that the partnership commits to upholding such principles as "providing support that promotes country ownership" (GPE, 2016a, p. 4). Finally, GPE includes private actors as core partners, with a separate constituency for companies and foundations on its board of directors and private participation within local education groups (LEGs) at the country level.

ECW was officially launched in May 2016 at the World Humanitarian Summit, but it represented the culmination of several years of mobilization toward a global fund targeted specifically to education in emergency contexts. ECW was largely spearheaded by Gordon Brown, UN Special Envoy for Global Education, and built on a 2016 report produced by ODI entitled *Education Cannot Wait: Proposing a Fund for Education in Emergencies* (ODI, 2016), which described it as "a fund designed to transform the global education sector for children affected by crises" (p. 7). As stated in its strategic plan, ECW seeks to "transform the aid system" with a new approach to educational aid that responds to the need for more flexible and rapid financing to education in settings of emergency; ECW focuses specifically on "speedy education responses in emergencies" and "quality of education for the long run" (ECW, 2018d, p. 8).

Financing education takes on a new level of urgency in contexts of crisis, where existing aid mechanisms are viewed as unable to respond in a timely and flexible way. ECW promotes collaboration and endeavors to foster joint efforts between stakeholders to address education in the contexts of emergency and protracted crises (ECW, 2018d). ECW's partnership structure promotes close collaboration to produce "collective effectiveness and better outcomes" (p. 8). A key aspect of ECW is its public–private structure, and an explicit goal of ECW is attracting new sources of financing with a strong focus on the private sector. At the time of writing, ECW has invested $134.5 million toward education in 19 countries affected by crisis (ECW, 2018a).

ECW's governance includes a High-Level Steering Group (HLSG) to "provide overall strategic direction . . . comprised of partner organizations, including heads of government and senior ministers from crisis-affected and donor countries, as well as heads of multilateral agencies, NGOs, and foundations" (ECW, 2018a). The HLSG comprises 17 voting members and one chair. Voting members represent donor countries, beneficiary countries, civil society, the private sector, private foundations, and UN/multilateral agencies. A Secretariat, hosted by UNICEF in New York, provides administrative and operational support. At the country level, ECW funding management involves "bringing together existing leadership and coordination groups as needed to make proposals and decisions regarding Platform support appropriate to the crisis" (ODI, 2016, p. 18).

ECW, moreover, puts forth "national ownership" as a core principle and "promotes the localization agenda," in which the organization put the active participation of affected communities, local governments, and stakeholders at the center of its policymaking and country-level processes (ECW, 2018d, p. 14). Such organizational principles reflect the wider development agenda shift toward increased southern participation and voice in decisionmaking.

CONCLUSION

This chapter has sought to lay the foundation for the argument that I will present throughout this book—simplistically put, that international aid to education must be viewed through the lens of the partnership era, in which actors are connected to one other, and these connections often do not reflect equitable relationships. Here, I have traced the historical trajectory to what I have described as an era of partnership in international aid, paying particular attention to the rise of multistakeholder arrangements in development and the conflation of partnership with private-sector engagement and the growth of private authority.

Scholars and practitioners alike have raised several critiques of partnerships, many of which will also be discussed and reinforced throughout this book. These relate largely to issues of power: how power is distributed, who wields influence and in what ways and the implications of these power dynamics.

CHAPTER 3

New Actors and Relationships in Aid to Education

Understanding Power in a Transnational, Partnership-Based Network

The international aid landscape has changed dramatically in recent years, with greater numbers of increasingly diverse actors involved, as well as new and more convoluted mechanisms through which aid is distributed. With this new environment comes a need to rethink how we conceptualize and visualize the aid system. If, as researchers and practitioners, we approach analyses of aid from the starting point of the traditional bilateral-recipient relationship, we are failing to grapple with the complexity of the current era and, as a result, cannot adequately nor accurately assess the role of power. In this chapter, I argue for a network conceptualization of aid, which I believe recognizes the complexity of relationships, including the prevalence of partnerships in this new context. While Chapters 4 and 5 offer qualitative findings that explore issues of power in individual partnerships, here I show how a network approach allows an empirical, quantitative analysis of power not only within partnerships, but across them.

I begin by delving more deeply into the changing nature of aid, detailing how various scholars have conceptualized this new era, and then argue for envisaging aid to education as a network. I also explore how the nature of power might play out within this network. Although some scholars might argue that a networked environment can mitigate inequities, I posit that networks are just as likely to reproduce existing hierarchies. I support this position by providing examples of various studies that apply network analysis to understanding power in international development and aid, including research that specifically analyzes educational partnerships.

THE CHANGING "ARCHITECTURE" OF DEVELOPMENT AID

Traditionally, international development has been depicted as an architecture or a system with clear boundaries, positionalities, and relational processes.

But, as Ramalingam aptly explains: "Today, we are dealing with what has been called a 'many-to-many' world of aid. There are more agencies using more money and more frameworks to deliver more projects in more countries with more partners. . . . Some have argued this messy confluence of intentions, actors, and activities does not deserve the label 'system'" (2013, p. 5).

Scholte and Söderbaum similarly discuss "the poly-centric . . . multi-actor condition of contemporary development policy processes" (2017, p. 7), explaining that several terms and concepts have risen to prominence, each of which attempts to capture the messiness of the new development era. Given that the label *system* no longer applies to international aid, scholars have attempted to conceptualize this new era of international development in ways that reflect the surge in actors and complex relationships, including the rise of partnerships.

For instance, in a report for the Center for Global Development, Severino and Ray (2010) address the "radical transformation in the number and kinds of actors involved" and the "dynamic processes of multi-actor convergence" in development aid (p. 2). They present the concept of "hypercollective action," explaining that due to "the rapidly increasing number of actors that take part in a given policy, hypercollective action is not just about there being many more actors around the table. These actors of international cooperation are also much more heterogeneous in size, structure, processes and objectives than before" (p. 12). Hypercollectivity, according to Severino and Ray, results from the expanding degree of complexity produced by this surge of actors and the deepened density of their relationships. This newly hypercollective action alters relationships within the aid architecture, wherein those who give funds either increasingly collaborate and coordinate with one another, or they do not, with impacts on the effectiveness of distribution. And global partnerships clearly exhibit this hypercollectivity as sites of such actions.

Along similar lines, Diane Stone describes the international policy domain as the "global agora," borrowing from the Athenian *agora*—a marketplace, but also a "space of assembly" for public and political debate and activity: "The idea of agora is used here to identify a growing global public space of fluid, dynamic, and intermeshed relations of politics, markets, culture, and society. This public space is shaped by the interactions of its actors—that is, multiple publics and plural institutions" (2008, p. 21). The global agora lacks the clean, systemlike characteristics often applied to international policy arenas of the past, but instead it is "a domain of relative disorder and uncertainty where institutions are underdeveloped and political authority unclear, and dispersed through multiplying institutions" (2008, p. 21).

Education scholars have also picked up on this change in landscape. McCowan and Unterhalter (2015) explain that in education, "we are entering a new era in the politics of global development—one that has been characterized as a period of 'hypercollective action'. . . . In this era, transnational actors are multiplying and developing new alliances" (p. 65), and

Complexity (of partnerships) but also of individual actors (+#'s)

these alliances include multistakeholder (MSP) global funds. In an article for Devex, Sophie Edwards (2018b) reviews the "excessive proliferation" of partnership-based funding mechanisms for education, raising the issue of fragmentation due to so many new players and pathways for financing education and development. For better or worse, the education sector's hypercollectivity is characterized by the participation of hundreds of organizations increasingly joining one another via various forms of partnerships.

The growing number of public and private actors joining global MSPs, where partners engage in collective policymaking and provide resources via vertical funding mechanisms, reflects the new hypercollective landscape and echoes Stone's global agora. And each of these ideas—hypercollectivity, global agora, polycentric—complement another concept gaining in popularity among both scholars and practitioners of development: the network.

networks

In her blog "From Architecture to Networks: Aid in a World of Variable Geometry," Minouche Shafik (2009) explains that what is commonly termed the international aid "architecture" is more aptly understood as a network. Stone (2008, p. 28) similarly posits that the global agora is comprised of networks, including knowledge networks, epistemic communities, and "global public policy networks" embodied in MSP partnerships. In their blog "Addressing the Overcomplexity of International Aid Architecture," Deutscher and Jacquet (2010) argue for an "overlapping networks approach" to understanding the myriad relationships between and the activities of actors engaged in international development. Ramalingam (2013) proposes that conceptualizing international aid as a network captures the "intricate webs of social, economic, technological, political, and ecological relationships that alternately drive or inhibit change" (p. 326). This chapter aims to show that international aid to education, as well as the partnership-based structure that increasingly characterizes it, can best be understood from a network perspective.

complexity networks

networks (history)

As I explain next, the study of networks in international relations is a relatively recent area of scholarship, which arose in response to perceived shortcomings of traditional analyses of international actors. Historically, research on the nature of interstate relationships assumed particular hierarchies and structures, based mainly on material resources or military clout. A network approach offers an alternative perspective and "defines structures as emergent properties of persistent patterns of relations among agents that can define, enable, and constrain those agents" (Hafner-Burton, Kahler, & Montgomery, 2009, p. 562). Through examining the structure of relationships, network analysis has shown that international relations can be understood as a complex arrangement in which actors' positions are constructed through relational processes, not solely through individual characteristics. And in the context of partnerships, these relational processes do not always produce equitable outcomes (Finnemore, 2014; Goddard, 2009; Hafner-Burton et al., 2009; Hughes, Peterson, Harrison, & Paxton, 2009; Kahler, 2009; Moaz, Terris, Kuperman, & Talmud, 2003).

UNDERSTANDING POWER IN NETWORKS

As Borgatti, Everett, and Johnson (2013, p. 2) describe: "Networks are a way of thinking about social systems that focus our attention on the relationships among the entities that make up the system." A widespread recognition of the need to conceptualize phenomena as networks has resulted in "an explosion of interest" in network analysis, including in international relations, education, and development studies (Borgatti et al., 2009, p. 892).

In education and development, scholars have applied the concept of a network to describe governance arrangements in which the introduction of nonstate actors has shifted the roles and activities of states. This shift from state-centric to a multiscalar environment has been termed *network governance* (Ball, 2009; McGrew, 2004). Similarly, links created through policymaking processes, also related to the new and evolving role of the private sector, have been described as *education policy networks* (Verger, 2012). And the concept of educational *knowledge networks* (also often termed *epistemic communities*) results from a new rise in global knowledge mobilization in education (Cooper, 2014; Menashy & Read, 2016; Read, 2019).

Researchers have approached the analysis of these varied forms of networks through a range of methodological tools, including network ethnography (Hogan, Sellar, & Lingard, 2016; Howard, 2002), and bibliometrics (Estabrooks et al., 2008; Goldie, Linick, Jabbar, & Lubienski, 2014). But the most common and well-established approach to analyzing networks is social network analysis (SNA), widely adopted in both the physical and social sciences (Borgatti et al., 2009). SNA allows researchers to understand which actors, or *nodes*, occupy the most central positions within a network, while also shedding light on the forms and strength of relationships between different actors, or *ties*. SNA also examines the overall structures of networks. Graphing techniques and software have enabled researchers to visualize the properties of networks, which include positionality, overall distribution, and density of the network (Borgatti et al., 2009, 2013).

Network analysis offers two key benefits to the study of the current era of partnerships. First, as I've reiterated throughout this book, the aid environment is messy, and growing more so with the rapid introduction of new players and partnership-based funding mechanisms in recent years. Network analysis allows those examining this environment to recast this messiness as complexity and study the roles, relationships, and interactions among all those included in this vast web of players. As Deutscher and Jacquet (2010) explain:

> If we accept that the multitude of actors, as well as the multitude of development challenges and needs make complexity an inevitable feature of development assistance, it follows that the aid "architecture" should not try either to

hide it or ignore it. . . . What is important is that all actors need to understand
their efforts not only in isolation, but take the context of this complexity into
account.

And network analysis allows researchers to embrace this complexity.
Ramalingam (2013), who endorses a "complex systems" approach to aid,
discusses how network analysis lets development actors better understand
their own positions within policy and practice environments, and also clari-
fies both the processes involved in aid distribution and areas needing attention within recipient countries (p. 301). He goes on to explain: "Social
network analysis power comes from how it can reveal the actors and relationships which are at the heart of development and humanitarian efforts"
(p. 324).

Second, and arguably more important, network analysis holds signifi-
cance in this era of partnership because it can capture the intricacies of
power dynamics, aligning them with the forms of power that I introduced in
Chapter 1. Certainly, conceptualizing the global aid landscape as a network
can generate both positive and negative interpretations. For instance, some
argue that networks engender more innovation, with an increased degree
of knowledge sharing (Shafik, 2009). Networks have "dynamited old practices, bringing additional funding as well as new capacities" (Severino &
Ray, 2010, p. 4), where "actors can also effectively contribute . . . working
together on joint objective through a networking approach" (Deutscher &
Jacquet, 2010; also see Reinicke, 1999).

Many scholars consider networks as flat spaces for the equitable exchange of information, ideas, and dialogue. In this sense, networks are "assumed to reduce power disparities among members, flattening exogenous
power asymmetries. . . . In this view, therefore, global networks, by their
nature, diminish the power of actors who would dominate outside the network" (Faul, 2016b, p. 187).

Some argue, however, that the positive assumption of network "flat-
ness" offers too simplistic an understanding of network structures and pathways, and that networks are also as likely to be inequitable and hierarchical
spaces (Faul, 2016b). Relationships within a network might produce depen-
dencies where some actors are reliant on others (Rhodes, 2007). As Stone
(2008) describes, and as I'll explain later in reference to several studies,
networks can produce the "dynamics for exclusion, seclusion, and division"
and might be

characterized primarily by elite rule and lack of participation . . . the different
varieties of networks that intersect and help compose public spaces can be a
force for democratization by creating a venue for representation of "stakeholder" interests, a means for wider participation in modes of global governance
and a venue for societal voices. In short, networks are "gateways." However,

these same networks can also be exclusive, elite and closed to deliberative decision making. (p. 22)

Stone (2008) also explains that participating in a network requires resources, including time and money, and highlights that therefore, participants from poorer countries face obstacles to active engagement. Thus, as Ramalingam (2013) puts it in reference to development aid, network analysis "suggests that the vertical linkages within social networks also have a strong influence on who receives international aid. . . . Position in the overall system really does matter" (p. 306).

Several scholars have argued that networks are theoretically just as likely to reproduce power asymmetries as they are to ameliorate them. Analysts have exposed such power hierarchies through different empirical approaches and conceptualized power in various ways, all through the unique lens of a network, showing that power is dependent on not only an actor's characteristics, but also its location within the network structure. As Hughes et al. (2009) explain: "Network analysis reveals how power is a function of the cohesiveness of groups within a given network" and "structures opportunity and exchange within networks" (p. 1717). For instance, an entity that has a high degree centrality measure (meaning many strong links to other actors or organizations) is likely to be relatively powerful because it can benefit from increased access to resources (Beckfield, 2008; Hafner-Burton et al., 2009). Hafner-Burton et al. (2009) note how centrality, moreover, can "shape the flow of information among nodes and alter common understandings of relative capabilities, common interests, or norms" (p. 570).

Power can also be illuminated through network analysis by identifying "network brokers," who act as political entrepreneurs in that they have exclusive ties to different types of actors that otherwise would not be connected. By acting as their sole link, the broker holds power through its *betweenness* and ability to control flows of information and resources. Actors that are marginal within the network, therefore, are dependent on these brokers (Hafner-Burton et al., 2009; Goddard, 2009).

Even those actors within a network that might appear on the surface to lack influence because of low degree centrality may in fact have power due to their *exit option*, where some have an ability to leave the network easily. Those nodes that may seem peripheral to the network have the power to "de-link," where "strategic efforts within the network to exploit bargaining power may result in threats of exit by those who are its targets" (Hafner-Burton et al., 2009, p. 571). Such marginal nodes that are not dependent on others in the network, which perhaps have ample resources or can benefit equally from engaging in options outside the network, therefore wield the power to exit. Understanding the characteristics of such nodes and their history of relationships within and outside the network helps to identify them as peripheral, yet powerful.

Although these conceptions of power apply different terms than those introduced in Barnett and Duvall's taxonomy of power (described in Chapter 1), they in fact complement and align very closely to the concept of structural power.

NETWORK RESEARCH ON INTERNATIONAL DEVELOPMENT AND AID

Prior research from the fields of international development, international relations, and education has used network analysis to show power hierarchies and unbalanced relationships empirically. Several studies that use network analysis to understand international relations have naturally focused on single intergovernmental organizations, such as the United Nations, European Union, or World Bank, as sole units of analysis (Beckfield, 2008; Hafner-Burton et al., 2009; Torfason & Ingram, 2010). But other studies have begun to examine the ways that global organizations link to one another and the potential inequities that manifest. For example, in their study *Power Positions: International Organizations, Social Networks, and Conflict*, Hafner-Burton and Montgomery (2006) question the premise that international organizations comprised of government members promote peace and equality. Through SNA, they find that intergovernmental agencies promote "hierarchies of prestige in the international system" and create "disparate distribution of social power" (p. 3).

Also studying intergovernmental organizations, Jason Beckfield's network analysis of "the world polity" examines and compares changes to organizations over time, and to their member-states, and shows that "prominent IGOs [Inter-Governmental Organizations] tend to be exclusive rather than universal in membership" (Beckfield, 2008, p. 437). Hughes et al. (2009) also apply the concept of world polity to understand global networks and examine power and inequality through the lens of international nongovernmental networks (INGOs) and their ties to states. Their SNA finds that some states are more central and densely tied to more INGOs, and so "powerful, more connected states are more likely to influence the norms and ideologies that INGOs use to create and disseminate their agendas" (p. 1733).

In education, recent literature has posited that private actors are now exercising authority in the policymaking arena via network governance, where educational challenges are increasingly addressed through partnerships of like-minded epistemic communities inclusive of businesses and corporate foundations (Ball, 2010, 2012; Ball & Junemann, 2012). It has been argued that such networks act as forums where "new voices and interests are represented in the policy process, and new nodes of power and influence are constructed or invigorated" (Ball, 2010, p. 155). Within these networked forums, therefore, policies on public education, its assessment, financing, and delivery are decided by both state and nonstate actors, often within transnational public–private arrangements and also at national levels (Ball, 2012; Ball & Junemann, 2012; Rizvi & Lingard, 2010).

A small number of studies have examined MSP partnerships using SNA, exposing issues of power and influence. For example, Schiffer and Waale's study of the MSP CGIAR's[1] work in Ghana applies SNA and "power-mapping" to understand "the influence/power of different actors" (2008, pp. 1–3). They arrive at the interesting finding that informal networks hold more perceived influence and relevance than formal relationships.

One of the few scholars to examine transnational partnerships in education rigorously using SNA is Moira Faul. In her 2016 study, Faul applies SNA to investigate if network relationships within the Global Partnership for Education (GPE) board of directors lessens or exacerbates asymmetries of power. In this research, she combines data from policy documents with key informant interviews to understand both formal and informal relationships within GPE, and she concludes that "relative power is bestowed unequally among network members" (Faul, 2016b, p. 193). And in their study *Power and Multistakeholderism: The Structuring of Spaces Between Fields*, Faul and Jordan Tchilingirian (2018) ask whether MSPs enable voices for all stakeholders or solidify existing power dynamics and the associated privileges. Using SNA, they examine the board membership of several MSPs that focus on different aspects of the Sustainable Development Goals (SDGs), including in the education sector. They arrive at the highly nuanced conclusion that the "ways in which different actors, interests, and field resources are mobilised into the partnership space between fields shapes the extent to which multistakeholderism may fulfil its normative promise to give meaningful voice to traditionally marginalized voices, or conversely intensify the risk of locking in the preferences of more powerful 'partners'" (Faul and Tchilingirian, 2018, p. 29).

Similar to Faul and Tchilingirian, Robin Shields and I wanted to understand power through the use of SNA, not only within an MSP, but across partnerships as well, and specific to the education sector. Next, I explain this study, its findings, and what this network analysis says about power hierarchies within an era of partnership in global education.

NETWORKS, PARTNERSHIPS, AND AID TO EDUCATION

As I explore hierarchies and influence in the context of partnership throughout this book, I focus on two main forms and manifestations of power: *structural power*, which operates by reinforcing the power of donors and multilaterals within partnerships, as well as an associated absence of southern influence; and *productive power*, where MSPs have served to produce and enable the private sector as a new player in global education policy through a particular aspirational discourse (Barnett & Duvall, 2005a). In our 2017 study, *Unequal Partners? Networks, Centrality, and Aid to International Education*, Shields and I used SNA to better understand power relationships among organizations involved in international educational development. Looking at networks of comembership in prominent international education partnerships, we mapped relations among different types of actors and observed patterns of relationships between them. We also examined how power operates by looking at positionality within the network, determining the extent to which centrality differs across organizations from the Global South and Global North. Later, I view these findings through the lens of structural and productive power.

Our primary data consisted of organizational membership lists in seven partnership-based organizations: the GPE, the Global Campaign for Education (GCE), the Inter-Agency Network for Education in Emergencies (INEE), the United Nations Girls' Education Initiative (UNGEI), the United Nations Global Education First Initiative (GEFI), the Global Business Coalition for Education (GBC-E), and the International Working Group on Education (IWGE).[2] The membership of these partnerships comprised 293 entities (actors or organizations), with each entity holding membership in between one and five partnerships.

We classified the member organizations into seven categories:

- *Bilateral donors* (24 organizations) include the United States Agency for International Development (USAID) and the United Kingdom's Department for International Development (DfID).
- *Businesses* (34 organizations) include companies such as Accenture, Cisco, and Chevron.
- *Civil society organizations (CSOs) or nongovernmental organizations (NGOs)* (140 organizations) are directly involved in program implementation in international development education, such as the Norwegian Refugee Council and Oxfam International. This category also includes advocacy campaigns and networks, as well as charities. Because this group is so large, we distinguish between those in northern (83 organizations) and southern (57 organizations) countries, using the classification described later in this chapter.
- *International organizations* (14 organizations) are those whose members are nation-states (Beckfield, 2008), such as UNICEF and international financial institutions such as the World Bank. The category includes multilateral development donors, such as the United Nations Development Programme (UNDP) and the European Commission.
- *Private foundations* (7 organizations) include any development donor that is not a national government, but that has a primary

purpose of funding other organizations, such as the Aga Khan Foundation and Open Society Foundation.

- *Recipient national governments* (60 governments) include such entities as the governments of Tanzania, Bangladesh, and Bolivia.
- *Universities and research institutes* (14 organizations) include entities such as the University of Sussex and the Brookings Institution. The focus of these organizations is research rather than program implementation.

For each entity, we identified the location of its headquarters and matched this location with the four World Bank income classifications (i.e., low, lower-middle, upper-middle, and high). On this basis, we were able to identify the possibilities for South/South and North/South relationships advocated by the Paris Declaration on Aid Effectiveness (OECD, 2005, p. 18). Based on this classification, we designated actors as either "northern" (i.e., from a high- or upper–middle-income country) or "southern" (i.e., from a lower- or lower–middle-income country), with the understanding, as discussed in Chapter 1, that these terms are imperfect and delineate broad socioeconomic categories that encapsulate a great deal of diversity and variation. We explored the geospatial distribution of the northern and southern organizations using the Google Geocoding application programming interface (API), which translates the text describing the location of the headquarters (e.g., "Geneva, Switzerland") into a geospatial coordinate (i.e., a latitude/longitude coordinate). Our analysis calculated and examined both the structure of the education partnership network and the degree of centrality of various entities. *Degree centrality* refers to "actors that are extensively involved in relationships with other actors" by determining a count of the ties to one another (Wasserman & Faust, 1994, p. 173).

Understanding the Educational Partnership Network

The educational partnership network includes a range of organizational types that span the state and nonstate sectors. Traditionally prominent aid actors (namely, state-based funders and recipients) are represented in the network with 24 bilateral donor agencies, 14 international financial institutions, and 60 recipient governments. The network membership, however, signifies the growth of nonstate actors participating in the global education policy landscape, with numerous CSOs—140, the most of any organizational type in the network—as well as 34 businesses and 7 private foundations. Also, 14 universities and research institutes are included in the network. Purely based on numerical counts, the network shows an expansion of representation beyond the traditional aid structure, with strong participation from the nonstate sector.

We found that many of the most central organizations are bilateral aid donors (see Table 3.1). For example, DfID, the Norwegian Agency for Development Cooperation (NORAD), and USAID all have high values, ranked second, third, and fourth for centrality. These agencies are members of five partnerships, which connect them to a large number of other organizations. The Australian Agency for International Development (AUSAID), Danish International Development Agency (DANIDA), the German development agency Gesellschaft für Internationale Zusammenarbeit (GIZ), and Swedish International Development Cooperation Agency (SIDA), all bilateral donors, are also among the 10 most central actors. The least central bilateral donors are China and Croatia, which are jointly ranked 245th (equally) in centrality and are members of only one partnership (see Tables 3.1–3.3). These cases suggest that donors with higher centrality

Table 3.1. Entities with the 20 Highest Degrees of Centrality

Entity Name	Type of Entity
1. Plan International	Civil society/NGO
2. USAID	Bilateral donor
3. NORAD	Bilateral donor
4. DfID	Bilateral donor
5. ActionAid International	Civil society/NGO
6. AUSAID	Bilateral donor
7. DANIDA	Bilateral donor
8. SIDA	Bilateral donor
9. GIZ	Bilateral donor
10. Netherlands Ministry of Development Cooperation	Bilateral donor
11. UNICEF	International organization
12. World Bank	International organization
13. UNESCO	International organization
14. GCE	Civil society/NGO
15. IBIS	Civil society/NGO
16. Oxfam International	Civil society/NGO
17. Save the Children	Civil society/NGO
18. Global Affairs Canada	Bilateral donor
19. European Commission	Bilateral donor
20. Open Society Foundation	Private foundation

Table 3.2. Entities with the 20 Lowest Degrees of Centrality

Entity Name	Type of Entity
275. ITWORX Education	Business
276. Kano	Business
277. Lenovo	Business
278. McKinsey & Co.	Business
279. Nestle	Business
280. NRS International	Business
281. Oando	Business
282. PricewaterhouseCoopers (PwC)	Business
283. Reed Smith	Business
284. Standard Chartered	Business
285. Sumitomo Chemical	Business
286. Tata Sons Ltd.	Business
287. Trans Javagas Pipeline	Business
288. Western Union	Business
289. Vitol Foundation	Private foundation
290. Cisco	Business
291. Camfed	Civil society/NGO
292. Care	Civil society/NGO
293. Leonard Cheshire Disability	Civil society/NGO
294. Commonwealth Secretariat	International organization

Table 3.3. Network Centrality Measures by Organizational Type

Organization Type	Degree Centrality
Businesses	−1.087
Bilateral donors	1.028
CSOs/NGOs (North)	−0.008
CSOs/NGOs (South)	0.444
International organizations	−0.141
Private foundations	−0.357
Recipient governments	0.030
University/research organizations	−0.692

For findings of regression analysis of centrality as an outcome of organization type and national GDP, see Menashy & Shields (2017), page 508.

measures, in particular agencies in the top 10 for centrality measures, are greater providers of international aid, committing larger budgets to overseas development assistance than those with lower values (OECD, 2016).

The geographic plot of organization locations (Figure 3.1A) shows that they represent a large distribution throughout the world. While there are concentrations of points (e.g., in Western Europe and the northeastern United States), there are few populated areas that are completely unrepresented, and there is consistent representation throughout the Global South (e.g., sub-Saharan Africa). However, when connections are shown between the points (Figure 3.1B), there is a much higher density of connections in the Global North than elsewhere, and there is little evidence of South–South connectivity, as there are few connections either across sub-Saharan Africa or between sub-Saharan Africa and the rest of the world.

The plot of locations (Figure 3.1A) shows that actors are distributed over most regions of the world. However, the plot of network ties (Figure 3.1B) shows that connections are unevenly distributed, with many ties to Europe and North America and relatively few ties between the southern countries.

Although low- and lower–middle-income countries are strongly represented in the network (second only to CSOs in total number), our analysis showed that recipient governments are less likely to hold central positions across partnerships. The five most central recipients (Bangladesh, Ethiopia, Guyana, and Mozambique), jointly ranked as 115th in centrality, are all members of the same two partnerships (GPE and UNGEI). Southern countries are not strongly connected to one another, as their connections primarily go North to South (see Figure 3.1B). Combined with the very high centrality measures of donors, these results indicate that aid recipients hold peripheral positions.

From these findings, we posited that the structure of the network reproduces power relationships that predate the discursive shift to partnership. Specifically, bilateral donors are the most central organizations in the partnership network, while recipient countries are less central. These findings suggested to us that donors are likely to shape the flows of information, ideas, and normative preferences of these partnerships. Despite the emergence of hypercollectivity, with a rhetorical emphasis equity between partners, the structure of the partnership network tends to reflect the established relationships and roles of aid actors.

Our analysis also showed that the private sector (most notably businesses) tend to have low integration into the partnership network; the least central organizations (tied for 245th) are Chevron, Exxon, Credit Suisse, McKinsey, and PwC, all of which are only members of the GBC-E. The involvement of the private sector appears, on the surface, to be relatively superficial. In terms of businesses and foundations, their marginal status

Figure 3.1A. World map plot of geographic locations of the organizations in this study.

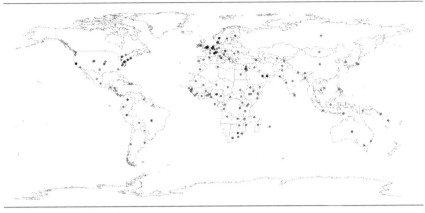

Figure 3.1B. World map plot of connections between the organizations in this study.

Source: Menashy and Shields (2017), p. 495–517. Reprinted with permission of Taylor & Francis Ltd, http://www.tandfonline.com.

in the network may be indicative of a wider lack of financial commitments from the private sector (van Fleet, 2011), which sees investments in education as difficult to track (Menashy, 2016), despite high-profile calls to increase private funding (Brown, 2016a; Rose & Steer, 2013; Sachs, 2015). It seems unlikely that the structure of partnership networks alone can explain the minimal levels of private-sector funding compared to other sectors.

A better explanation, we posit, is that the peripheral status of the private sector is symptomatic of a larger lack of financial engagement in the education sector because the private companies have an *exit option*, in that international educational development does not often constitute part of their core activities and is only minimally required to maintain some level of legitimacy. In the context of declining bilateral aid to education, our results suggested to us that the network of partnerships needs the private sector more than the private sector needs to be part of the network. In this way, private actors are being brought into the network as invited or solicited actors based on a discourse promoting their expertise and added value. Such invitations, which often seek to elicit funding from the private sector, in fact are more likely instead to allow businesses a place at the policy table regardless of resource contributions. In this way, I argue that inclusion of the private sector embodies a form of productive power, which later chapters discuss in more detail.

Interestingly, CSOs in both the North and South are very numerous and highly central, with southern CSOs holding more central positions in the network overall. CSOs have long been central to the promotion of education as a humanitarian act and consistent purveyors of rights-based approaches, offering a normative and moral element to the promotion of education, so civil society participation within transnational partnerships arguably affords advocacy and legitimacy. CSO network positionality enables advocacy and influence that simultaneously and ambiguously combine the embracing of nonstate actors in development with grassroots activism and democratic participation (Kamat, 2004).

To summarize, our study showed empirically the importance of separating the rhetorical collectivity and collaboration characteristic of partnerships from assumptions of egalitarianism; using SNA, Shields and I argued that the shift toward partnership perpetuates rather than transforms power relationships in international development education. In particular, donors preserve a position within the network suggesting that they would maintain the greatest influence over both the resource flows and normative preferences of partnerships. Additionally, our study observed the growing power of private actors as policymakers—but as I will argue, not as funders. The research literature has demonstrated that private actors are increasingly involved in international education networks (including in GPE and ECW, as will be seen later in this book), and our exploration of those participating in these networks empirically confirms a significant presence of businesses and foundations. However, our analysis shows that the integration of the private sector is relatively weak.

CONCLUSION

This chapter illustrated the changing nature of development aid and how various scholars have attempted to conceptualize this new environment. Such concepts—hypercollectivity, a global agora, polycentric, and multiscalar—are all complemented by the notion of international aid as a network. A network conception is apt because it speaks to the complexity of this new architecture, showing both its nature—including the range of types and increasing number of actors within it—and its expansive, interconnected structure. What is more, network analysis allows us to see, empirically, that the environment is far from equitable. In fact, networks are often hierarchical, with entities embodying various degrees of power and influence.

Furthermore, when examining partnerships as interconnected within a network, we can see a visual structure that indicates the reproduction of power asymmetries. These imbalances manifest within partnerships, as seen through network studies of MSP partnerships, but also across partnerships due to cross-membership. Visualizing and analyzing partnerships as a network tell us a great deal about educational aid, including the range of types of actors, the strength of and different kinds of relationships, and which entities wield power.

I argue that when analyzed in terms of a network, structural power emerges as dominant in educational partnerships. Such power manifests within a network, where actors are often positioned in a hierarchy, and such positionality means that their capacities are being constituted. In other words, partnerships, when viewed as embedded within a wider network, are clearly spaces in which particular actors wield influence (donors), while others do not (recipients). The high-degree centrality of donors and multilaterals, as well as the low-degree centrality of recipients, indicates a clear power differential based on the potential for influence. Also, the dominance of aid flows from North to South, and the near absence of South-to-South ties between countries displays the maintenance of traditional aid relationships.

Despite changes to the aid architecture that endeavored to move away from compulsory power and conditionalities, the same donor–recipient power hierarchy appears to have been reproduced within the network, in contrast to rhetorical shifts that indicate otherwise. The structure is maintained, allowing those with wealth and resources to retain their positions relative to others.

Productive power, which results from the diffusion of discourse, is more challenging to observe using network analysis methods. Yet, I will argue based on these findings, triangulated with the qualitative analyses to come in Chapters 4 and 5, that the proliferation of private actors within the aid network represents a form of productive power. As will be detailed in upcoming chapters, partnership arrangements reflect a legitimizing of the private sector under the discursive pretense of improving and advancing the work of traditional state-based aid organizations, resting on normalized assumptions relating to their expertise and legitimate knowledge. Further, as I will show through qualitative case studies in Chapters 4 and 5, partnerships primarily invite private actors into partnerships to make contributions as much-needed financiers. In this sense, the network needs the private sector for its resources, but private actors show reluctance to participate as funders. And so they have the power to exercise their exit option.

NOTES

1. CGIAR was formerly known by its full name, the Consultative Group for International Agricultural Research.

2. As noted in Chapter 1, the Education Cannot Wait Fund (ECW) was not included in this analysis because its full membership list was not publicly available at the time of this research.

CHAPTER 4

Power Dynamics in a Multistakeholder Fund

The Case of the Global Partnership for Education

Few organizations better exemplify a shift toward partnership-based mandates as the Global Partnership for Education (GPE). Inclusive of stakeholders from the Global North and South, representing governments, United Nations (UN) agencies, and the nonstate sector, the GPE is underpinned by an idea that the design and implementation of education and development policies are strengthened via collaborative, coordinated partnership arrangements.

Yet as this chapter will describe, the case of GPE shows that despite an effort to address critiques of international aid through the establishment of a new organization that aims to increase equity and participation in the development process, those who have historically held power have retained their hierarchical positioning due to the GPE's decisionmaking, administrative, and aid distribution structure. The existence of structural power serves to maintain the existing North/South power hierarchy that the partnership was designed to ameliorate. I also discuss the ways in which GPE has made significant efforts to include southern participation in the face of these structural challenges.

GPE, moreover, presents an interesting case of private-sector engagement, in which business and philanthropic, foundation actors have participated in policy spaces through governance, but without deep engagement and with nominal funding commitments. This chapter explains and untangles the complex roles of private actors in GPE.[1]

THE HISTORY AND MANDATE OF THE GLOBAL PARTNERSHIP FOR EDUCATION

The GPE began as the Education for All (EFA) Fast Track Initiative (FTI), launched in 2002 by the World Bank as a partnership predominantly comprised of donors—high-income bilateral agencies—to fund low-income countries and put them on a fast track toward universal primary education. The FTI came under criticism in the late 2000s, leading to an organizational overhaul and rebranding into the current GPE. In large part, the restructuring was done in response to a 2010 external review of the organization that cited several major shortcomings to its governance, including the dominance of donors as decisionmakers. The legitimacy of the FTI was questioned and depicted as a funding organization driven by the Steering Committee, a small group comprised primarily of bilateral actors from the Global North:

> The FTI has been (and despite some modifications still is) an unbalanced partnership. Although described from the outset as a partnership and a compact, it was a donor initiative, with very little involvement of partner countries in its design, and it has remained more a donor collaboration than a genuine partnership. Partner countries, in particular, still have a very limited role and are not involved in financial decisions. (Cambridge Education, Mokoro, & Oxford Policy Management, 2010, p. xx)

The decisionmaking process was not adequately inclusive of recipient-country voices, and interview respondents who were involved with the FTI supported the claim that the Steering Committee was very "donor-centric" (personal communication, Secretariat, September 24, 2014) and was informally constituted to favor those actors with social capital or material wealth: "Often, if somebody would join the Steering Committee and the person had a very strong character or brought in a lot of money or something, that could shape the direction of the Initiative" (personal communication, Secretariat, August 15, 2014). The governance of the FTI was widely criticized as undemocratic and misaligned with participatory ideals.

The initiative was also inextricably tied to the World Bank. Many FTI staff had been employed in the Bank's education sector, the initiative was essentially considered a subunit of the Bank as a trust fund, and it was physically housed within the Bank's headquarters. As a respondent from the Secretariat at that time described: "When FTI was created, the World Bank, of course, was running the show" (personal communication, Secretariat, September 14, 2014). The Bank's prominent role fed criticisms of the FTI as simply perpetuating Bank education policy prescriptions. In 2008, for instance, the Global Campaign for Education (GCE) stated that "the World Bank has played an increasingly problematic role vis-à-vis the EFA Fast Track Initiative" and accused the FTI of prescribing "ideologically-driven policy advice" in line with World Bank mandates (2008, pp. 2, 9). The midterm external review also expressed concerns about the FTI's relationship to the Bank, stating it was "too dependent on the World Bank" (Cambridge Education et al., 2010, p. xxi).

The restructuring of the FTI into the GPE aimed to respond to these critiques, seeking to more explicitly give recipient countries and southern actors a voice in decisionmaking processes, as well as to break from its entwined relationship to the World Bank.

The FTI's rebranding into the GPE and its new membership structure transformed the organization into the largest multistakeholder partnership (MSP) in education, now governed by a diverse, constituency-based board of directors that includes 19 voting members representing donor countries, recipient countries, multilateral agencies, civil society organizations (CSOs), and the private sector and foundations. The GPE also includes 70 developing-country partners (DCPs) that receive resources via the GPE Fund, a pooled fund financed predominantly by northern-country partners of the GPE, from which disbursements are made to countries. To date, GPE has allocated over $4 billion to its DCPs (GPE, 2016a, 2016b, 2016c, 2018b).

The GPE is explicitly grounded in the Paris Declaration on Aid Effectiveness, as made clear in the GPE Charter:

> The Global Partnership is underpinned by principles set out in the March 2005 Paris Declaration on Aid Effectiveness. . . . Donors, multilateral agencies, CSOs and the private sector and private foundations then commit to aligning their support for a developing country partner's program. (GPE, 2013a, p. 3)

The GPE's governance structure, where all members are rhetorically defined as equal partners, is reflective of the Paris principles. Its financing arrangements and decisionmaking processes, inclusive of local actors within recipient countries and based on country-owned policies, also signify the goal of equal partnership. The organization is committed to "a country-led process" through which DCPs "take the lead on delivery" (GPE, 2016c, p. 6). One of the core guiding principles listed in its Charter is "country ownership and nationally identified priorities" (GPE, 2018a, p. 3). Its strategic plan similarly states that the partnership is committed to upholding such principles as "providing support that promotes country ownership" and "acting on our belief that inclusive partnership is the most effective means of achieving development results" (GPE, 2016c, p. 4).

Findings show, however, that such pronouncements are questionable in light of the historically constituted role of the World Bank as a host and Grant Agent,[2] the influential positions of high-income bilateral actors that fund education in recipient countries, and the privileging of dominant languages. Notwithstanding notable efforts to counter power asymmetries and elevate southern voices, structural power clearly manifests within the GPE due to the maintenance of hierarchies between actors as perpetuated through wealth, administrative roles, logistical constraints, and language, retaining the inequities that the partnership was designed to ameliorate.

POWER DYNAMICS IN THE GLOBAL PARTNERSHIP FOR EDUCATION

The Power of Those "Putting in the Money"

Donors from the Global North are widely perceived as holding power in the GPE as decisionmakers within countries and in governance. In-country participation of aid recipients is a staple of GPE processes, where local actors are asked to contribute actively to the local education groups (LEGs)—collaborative, country-level forums involved in a variety of GPE-related activities, including policy design, implementation, and monitoring. According to interviews, however, local stakeholder participation in LEGs is limited in many contexts. Respondents highlighted a lack of participation by local actors within the LEGs and a more dominant representation of bilateral donors: "We have what we call like a 'country-driven model' . . . the idea of a LEG. That's really like an ideal concept, and the reality is very messy . . . the LEG may actually be really strongly donor-focused" (personal communication, Secretariat, August 14, 2014). As a respondent argued: "There needs to be a better gathering of representation in these local education groups" (personal communication, CSO, March 7, 2014). Local participation is uncertain, given that within the country, international funders are said to be in dominant positions in the decisionmaking arena.

The GPE touts its funding process as country owned, where funding applications include an ostensibly country-designed and written Education-Sector Plan (ESP). These plans, however, are likely not solely country driven, and they arguably reflect the agendas of those aid actors that hold influence within recipient countries, primarily those that are funders of national education systems. Interviewees described the ESP-design process as involving a range of national and international actors: "It's usually a dialog that will start between the key funders, external funders of the education system and the government" (personal communication, Secretariat, September 14, 2014). Bilateral agencies in particular were identified as exercising a great deal of influence, specifically those who are large contributors of aid to a particular country: "I would think about who the largest donor is in the sector, because they may have more substantive influence on the broader policy. . . . [GPE] doesn't actually drive the policy" (personal communication, Secretariat, January 23, 2015).

ESPs, moreover, face a quality assurance process through which external consultants, trained by the GPE Secretariat, assess whether the plan meets particular standards. Critics have questioned this process, asking if it counters country ownership of education policy. For instance, a recipient country representative reportedly raised this critique at a board meeting, stating that an ESP is "not GPE property" and that "it is sovereign property . . . and it should be driven by criteria and conditions of the country's sector" (personal communication, UN/multilateral agency, September 20, 2018).

As a respondent explained: "The essence that developing-country governments are on equal footing with the donors is a very good foundation, but it's not the reality at the moment. Partly because of the way in which things are framed, and the disproportionate power that's given to people who have been putting in the money" (personal communication, CSO, January 13, 2014).

Funders also wield influence at the governance level of the partnership. The bilateral agencies of high-income countries on the board—the primary donors to the GPE—have the most dominant voice. One board member said, "I think donors sometimes have clearly a disproportionately influential voice, and I think that that is a problem" (personal communication, CSO, January 14, 2014). Others agreed: "[I]t's those with the biggest financial status that probably have the loudest voice" (personal communication, foundations/private sector, February 4, 2014); "I think definitely that those who fund the GPE get a lot of the attention" (personal communication, UN/multilateral agency, March 3, 2014); "donors are the most active on the board" (personal communication, recipient country, September 23, 2014). Another more specifically identified power as being held by "the donor countries. It would be, for example, UK, EU, the Netherlands too, the Danish used to, the Scandinavians as well. And Australia. These are the main ones. Those are the strong voices that are really steering the discussion" (personal communication, CSO, March 7, 2014).

Although efforts have been made in recent years to elevate southern voices in GPE governance (as I detail later in this chapter), the input and influence of DCPs are "still very weak . . . there's still work to be done on the [DCP] voices" (personal communication, CSO, September 12, 2018).

The ostensible goal of its constituency-based board of directors is to allow equal input into policy discussions, regardless of material resources, in order to cultivate "broad participation by all partners" and thus allow the GPE to operate as a genuine partnership (GPE, 2013a, p. 3). From the perspectives of respondents, however, the donor countries have the most dominant voice in decisionmaking, and this influence is clearly tied to their roles as financiers of the partnership. In spite of the MSP arrangement of the GPE, the aid provision decisions remain in the hands of high-income–country governments, much as was the case in the donor-centric FTI.

The roles of funders to the GPE are reflective of structural power due to the maintenance of a hierarchical relationship between those with wealth—providers of aid—and those who are in need, as recipients. Much as in a traditional aid relationship, donors exercise power via the wielding of resources, while recipients have much lower participation in decisionmaking. Despite organizational reforms and an explicit focus by stakeholders and its Secretariat on southern participation, including both DCP representatives and civil society, the GPE retains an aid distribution and decisionmaking structure in which funders occupy a structurally dominant position above recipients.

The Power of the World Bank

The organization repeatedly identified as having an outsized influence on the GPE process is the World Bank. The Bank has assumed multiple roles within the GPE: host to the GPE Secretariat, the official employer of GPE staff, a trustee of GPE funds, a member of the board of directors, a partner within LEGs, and its default Grant Agent (Evans, 2012; World Bank, 2014). Findings indicate that the Bank's current role is based upon its historically constituted, inextricable tie to the partnership. Because the FTI's embeddedness within the World Bank organization was so widely criticized, the restructuring sought to redefine this relationship. Since the rebranding of the FTI into the GPE, efforts have been made to maintain a more arms-length affiliation to the Bank. But concerns have persisted. For example, a group of global CSOs articulated in a report that "the hosting of the Secretariat within the World Bank and the reliance on the World Bank at country level create problems with autonomy, accountability, conflicts of interest, displacement of funds, bureaucracy and the GPE's identity as a partnership" (GCE & Oxfam, 2012).

As a result of such concerns, the GPE's association with the World Bank was assessed with a 2012 Hosting Review, which evaluated the Bank's role as physical host to the Secretariat and as an employer of its staff. Given the potential risks involved in a break from the Bank, this review suggested maintaining the hosting relationship, but implementing some reforms to ensure greater GPE autonomy (Evans, 2012). The decision to retain the World Bank–GPE relationship was based primarily on the fact that the Bank had historically played this role and that establishing a new hosting arrangement would be costly and time consuming and cause logistical problems that could threaten the partnership's progress. As recommended in the Hosting Review: "What the GPE Secretariat needs now is some certainty to get on with the job" (Evans, 2012, p. 22), suggesting the importance of continuity.

According to respondents, however, some partners were "not at all pleased" with the Hosting Review's outcome, as they expressed a desire for a more formal and clear separation from the World Bank (e.g., personal communication, CSO, March 3, 2014). Several respondents questioned Secretariat staff loyalty to the GPE as World Bank employees, as well as the Secretariat's independence to make decisions that might counter the Bank's views on educational priorities and policies.

The World Bank initiated what is now GPE, and it retains a central administrative role as host, which critics noted could impede the independence of the GPE and reinforce the power of the Bank to drive GPE agendas. The Bank, therefore, holds a position within the partnership that could hinder the GPE from changing and impede alternative actors from influencing the work of the Secretariat. In this way, the Bank wields structural power as a host to the GPE, a position that it holds in part due to its history with the FTI.

The World Bank's role as Grant Agent for the majority of recipient countries also reflects structural power, positioning the Bank as a highly influential player in the GPE country-level process. Each GPE grant is disbursed and monitored by a Grant Agent that distributes the funds at the country level, and in roughly 70 percent of cases, this role is filled by the World Bank (GPE, 2018b). As a Secretariat staff member explained: "I mean, if you're the supervising entity [Grant Agent], you have a lot of influence, whoever you are" (personal communication, August 15, 2014).

As described by some interviewees, the relationship to the World Bank is necessary, as the Bank is considered the only agency holding the fiduciary and logistical capacity—both globally and nationally—to maintain GPE processes: "[T]he actual oversight, the direct fiduciary oversight, and support, and capacity building, and safeguards are carried out by the supervising entity [Grant Agent]" (personal communication, Secretariat, September 15, 2014); "[i]t's a strange relation somewhat but I think in the circumstances, there's no other option" (personal communication, bilateral donor, May 20, 2014). Another described the "international status of the World Bank" as "somebody that you can call on if there's a need" (personal communication, Secretariat, September 15, 2014).

The Bank's role as Grant Agent is a core administrative position, which alongside its hosting role has been historically determined, as it was the implementer of funds for the FTI: "the Bank's extensive role as supervising entity [Grant Agent] is as much a function of FTI's history . . . as anything else" (Evans, 2012, p. 8). Along with its hosting role, several interviewees identified the Bank's Grant Agent status as problematic: "we tend to see a predominance of one organization's view right across. I think that's still a problem for the GPE. The World Bank, the dependency issue, is still a major issue" (personal communication, CSO, March 3, 2014). And, put more plainly by an in-country respondent, "I feel the Bank as a supervising entity [Grant Agent] has sometimes used [its role] to forward their own agency's agenda" (personal communication, UN/multilateral agency, June 19, 2014). Recent follow-up interviews explained that the debate concerning World Bank hosting continues: "The Bank is still the dominant supervising entity [Grant Agent] . . . I think that's really problematic" (personal communication, CSO, June 7, 2017). In discussing both its hosting and grant agent status, one respondent stated, "I think the issues with the World Bank are at an all-time high" (personal communication, CSO, September 12, 2018).

The historically constituted administrative role of the World Bank has allowed it to retain its position of power over the directions taken by the Secretariat as host, and over the aid distribution processes as Grant Agent. The Bank's significant responsibilities within the GPE reflect structural power, as the agency retains an influential and privileged hierarchical position relative to other actors, in particular recipient countries and their representatives. The Bank's dominant position within the GPE has substantively

determined its capacity to wield influence over both the Secretariat and recipient countries. A historically constituted hierarchy is maintained, benefiting the Bank through the maintenance of administrative roles.

Logistics, Language, and the Capacity to Engage

Actors from the Global North are seen overall as more actively engaged
and influential within the GPE, further contrasting the intention of having a
balanced partnership with southern actors. Notably contributing to unequal
participation are language barriers, where many governmental and nonstate
actors from the Global South are unable to communicate effectively. The
board members predominantly speak English, and circulated GPE documents are translated into only English and French. Over a third of GPE recipient countries do not have English or French as an official language. Yet,
as a respondent representing a southern organization explained, although
the GPE works "with governments that speak Portuguese and Spanish and
all kinds of languages . . . they do not translate any documents to other
languages other than French and English" (personal communication, CSO,
March 4, 2014).

Language barriers limit direct participation in discussions and affect the
confidence of some to express viewpoints on GPE directions. A board member from a northern agency stated: "I would much rather see much more effort and support put into helping people who are sitting in those [Southern]
seats, to really engage their constituency, and for them to feel more confident
to assert their voice than I think is sometimes the case" (personal communication, CSO, January, 2014). Another GPE partner described the challenge
of "figuring out how to best engage and mobilize the Southern constituencies because they're not as engaged as they could be . . . of course you have
language issues . . ." (personal communication, private sector/foundation,
February 4, 2014). A Secretariat staff member agreed: "There's much more
complex barriers to an effective representation of Southern members . . . I
think for the Southern board members, it's a lot harder language-wise . . ."
(personal communication, Secretariat, August 15, 2014).

Structural power is arguably reproduced in the GPE via "linguistic imperialism," a concept that accounts for the "hierarchisation" of languages
where colonial languages dominate and are imposed upon others (Phillipson,
1997, p. 238; Pennycook, 2000). Moreover, scholars have posited language
as a form of capital that holds economic value, signifying the wielding of influence and power (Hamid, 2016; Pennycook, 2000). In the case of the GPE,
the sole use of English and French in spoken discussions and circulated
documents reflects structural power in privileging those languages mastered
by the majority of northern board members, consistent with "the global hierarchy of languages" (Hamid, 2016, p. 268). Those from the Global South
who speak other languages—including widely spoken Portuguese, Spanish,

and Arabic, and many national languages such as Vietnamese, Urdu, Uzbek, Mongolian, Lao, and Khmer—are at a disadvantage in communication and less able to utilize their voices in decisionmaking spaces. A linguistic hierarchy retains those from the Global North in positions of power to influence the direction of GPE.

The issue of language relates to resource constraints, as some respondents explained that to translate each document into all languages would be enormously labor intensive and time consuming for the Secretariat. Resources also create barriers for southern actors, who have fewer human resources to dedicate to GPE engagement. As a board member explained, "[E]ngagement is really possibly more of a product of the capacity and the teams behind [the donors]," and so "donors have a more direct ear to the Secretariat" because of the presence of staff within donor agencies dedicated to GPE communication (personal communication, CSO, September 12, 2018). Preparation for board meetings involves at times the review of several hundred pages of documents, and donors have a bigger team devoted to reviewing and preparing for board meetings and engagement. Constituency sizes also affect engagement. Donor board members represent far fewer constituents than those of DCPs, making logistics, coordination, and communication among members more challenging for the DCPs (GPE, 2018b). The range and size of constituents complicate communication and board meeting preparation.

Efforts Toward an Equitable Partnership

GPE stakeholders indeed have made significant strides toward elevating southern voices. Several respondents described GPE as in fact being far more participatory than most other funding sources to education and development: "[I]t does a better job than pure bilateral foreign aid or foreign aid that is sort of a club of donors deciding their priorities and funding those priorities without input" (personal communication, CSO, June 7, 2017). As an example, southern CSOs have grown increasingly engaged on the GPE board through explicit efforts designed to promote their participation. The Secretariat and northern CSOs have supported regular calls between constituency members, sharing of materials, development of written input into board decisions, and preboard meetings to prepare for discussions and votes. As I was told: "[I]t's still common for Southern Civil Society to be quiet on some items. But I'll say, by and large, we have increased voice" (personal communication, CSO, September 12, 2018).

The donor-supported German BACKUP Initiative for Education in Africa represents another effective effort toward increasing southern participation. Since 2011, the initiative has directly supported African GPE partners with "quick, flexible, and demand-oriented support" in filling gaps between GPE funding applications and disbursements, allowing developing countries to apply for and use resources (GIZ, 2018). As an example, were the GPE to fund the construction of schools, BACKUP might step in to help fund an architect to design the school buildings and campus. At this time, BACKUP has supported over 180 applications from GPE African DCPs.

Similar to the southern CSOs, BACKUP began to support preboard meetings of the African constituencies: "They can sit together for three days, go through the board document, what makes it be decided, agree on whatever, and equip their board member to go with an opinion. And when they then went to the next board meeting, they were suddenly speaking out which was a huge change" (personal communication, bilateral donor, October 25, 2018). Based on this success, the Secretariat now supports the communication and preboard meetings of all GPE DCPs.

Respondents, however, questioned the genuine value of Secretariat-driven preboard meetings, where a board member critiqued the DCP meetings arranged by the Secretariat: "The Secretariat wants to do a good job of supporting those meetings as much as possible, but at this point, it may have gone too far in that direction, whereby the Secretariat sets the agenda, presents, facilitates discussion, and controls the entire day. So there have been [issues] of, are these even the right agenda items when you look at the GPE preboard meeting? Are they really focusing on the right issues? Are they really given the space to speak freely and decide on themselves? Or is it very much a GPE Secretariat focal point that is presenting on those work streams, and very much strictly articulating what their position is and, in a way, trying to convert the DCPs onto whichever position of the issue that they want. So there is that risk there" (personal communication, CSO, September 12, 2018). And DCPs, indeed, expressed concerns relating to "a validity to speak very freely" (personal communication, recipient country, October 2, 2017).

North/South Power Hierarchies Within GPE

Overall, the GPE structure retains a familiar power dynamic, with actors from the Global North more able to voice positions and steer decision-making than their southern counterparts. The key factors reinforcing this hierarchy are historically constituted administrative roles, the wielding of funds, and the ability to speak dominant languages, maintained through GPE decisionmaking and aid distribution structure. As the case of GPE has shown, in spite of attempts to reform the partnership into a more participatory sphere, power asymmetries remain, where those that in the past held positions of power have retained their dominant hierarchical standing. Actors collaborate under the pretenses of equity in decisionmaking, but those who hold historically constituted administrative positions, have material resources, and speak dominant languages, are situated differently within the partnership relative to others, and as a result have a stronger capacity to influence the direction of the organization. In spite of efforts toward southern, local participation (at both the governance and country levels), it is clear that organizations from the Global North have retained positions of power. This maintenance of the North/South aid hierarchy opposes the very goals that the GPE was established to reach.

Through the lens of the GPE, this case reveals the nature of structural power in exposing the structural inequities that continue to exist in the global education policy arena. Due to the proliferation of actors and the rise in complex collective action targeting educational development over recent decades, power is arguably less directly coercive than in the structural adjustment era of the 1980s and 1990s, as described in Chapter 2. Yet the identification of structural power in GPE exposes the reproduction of inequities that clearly conflict with the goals of partnership.

The GPE case holds implications for global policymaking, spurring questions as to the value of new partnership-based initiatives, in particular the establishment of MSP agencies. The case of the GPE, therefore, can inform international development aid programs more generally, beyond the field of education, where ideals of partnership and participation are grounded in an impetus for actors from the Global South to participate more explicitly in determining those policies that most affect them. Yet through their location in the aid hierarchy, some actors are determined to have more agency and capacity to drive the development agenda and in-country processes. In the case of the GPE, actors from the Global North, in particular donors and the World Bank, are positioned to maintain their power, while those from the Global South are structurally maintained in subjugated positions. Other MSP partnerships appear to fall prey to similar dynamics, including both within education—as will be seen in Chapter 5's case study of the Education Cannot Wait Fund (ECW)—and outside the education sector.

THE EMPOWERING OF PRIVATE ACTORS IN THE GLOBAL PARTNERSHIP FOR EDUCATION

As discussed in Chapter 2, the roles of private actors and their growing engagement in global education have raised several criticisms. In particular, scholars have questioned the degree of legitimacy and authority that the private sector has been granted within partnerships. In my research on GPE, I investigated the roles of both private foundations and companies to understand their relationships and influence, uncovering a complex interplay of actors and circumstances. I present GPE as a case in which private actors indeed have been empowered to enter a decisionmaking space but have not engaged in the manner desired by most other GPE stakeholders.

The Evolving Roles of Private Actors in the Global
Partnership for Education

At this time, the GPE board includes four seats for the nonstate sector, including three for CSOs and one for private actors. The private-sector/foundation constituency includes over 20 members, the majority of which are representatives from foundations with overarching educational mandates, including such prominent organizations as the Open Society Foundation, Hewlett Foundation, and Mastercard Foundation. Companies represent a smaller number of members, but they include large businesses such as Microsoft and Pearson Education.

The participation of private actors in GPE evolved differently for companies and for foundations. Early on, the foundations were seen as important to the partnership, as they held a capacity for innovation, particularly in terms of financing. One of the major critiques of the FTI was its insufficient funding to conflict-affected and fragile states, as FTI financing stipulated that countries must have a "sound education sector plan"—a challenge to develop for those countries experiencing crisis (Cambridge Education et al., 2010; Menashy & Dryden-Peterson, 2015; World Bank, 2005, p. 5). Because the partnership was therefore unable to fund many countries, which, due to their fragility, did not have strong education plans in place, there was a widespread "recognition that the FTI as it was, was not fit for purpose" (personal communication, private sector/foundation, February 4, 2014).

Interviewees recall how this lack of ability to support fragile states spurred an increased understanding of the value that the knowledge and experiences of private actors could bring. One respondent gives an account of a situation in 2007 where a postconflict country was unable to secure funding from the FTI and alternatively was supported by a country-specific pooled fund that combined contributions from one donor, one multilateral agency, and one foundation, and this mechanism was spearheaded in many ways by the expertise of the foundation. When the FTI began its restructuring, this pooled funding mechanism shed light on the expertise of foundations to better support education in fragile contexts, bringing to the forefront the value that a private source might bring to the partnership.

Up until this time, private foundations had very little engagement with the FTI, whereas companies were participants on the Steering Committee, represented by a member of the World Economic Forum: "There was no space at all. Private foundations had not been engaged at all. Now it could be my own interpretation. but I think because of the [postconflict country] experience and how engaged we'd been, and also around that time I think the role of private foundations in global education was becoming more recognized or appreciated, I think there was a recognition that [foundations] were significant players that essentially needed to be coordinated as well" (personal communication, private sector/foundation, February 4, 2014).

Inclusion of foundations into the GPE, therefore, was in large part a result of acknowledging the limitations of the FTI, where a problematic feature of the FTI was its inflexible funding policies, and was based on a growing discourse around the value of engaging foundations as significant players with particular expertise and experience.

Before the restructuring, therefore, a push was occurring to be more inclusive of foundations. The late 2000s also saw increasing partnerships between donor governments and foundations more generally, including various contracts and coordinated grants. And so when the decision was made to restructure the FTI into the GPE and employ a constituency-based board model, foundations were included in the conversation.

A small group of foundation representatives—each of whom had a previous relationship with the FTI—came together to gather a list of other foundations that were open to participating on the GPE board as members of a stand-alone "private foundation" constituency. Concurrently, a representative from the World Economic Forum formulated a separate list of companies, and a proposal was put forward to form two separate seats: one for the foundations and another for the private sector (i.e., companies). However, the new constituency model in the end included only one seat for the private sector/foundations—combining both companies and philanthropies—arguably due to a desire for keeping the board at a manageable size and assumptions that actors associated with corporate entities ought to be grouped together.

A second rationale for the inclusion of a private-sector/foundation seat was an understanding that corporate actors were becoming increasingly involved in educational policy debates and commonly addressed global educational issues within their corporate social responsibility (CSR) programs, and so engaging with companies was seen as making strides to solidify a relationship with an ostensibly important stakeholder in education. As an interviewee described: "I think it was in anticipation of the fact that there's just a greater and greater emphasis on the role of the private sector" (personal communication, Secretariat, August 14, 2014). And finally, from very early on, incorporating both foundations and companies into GPE was driven by a belief, based on experiences in the health sector, that private-sector actors would likely become a major financial resource in contributions to the GPE Fund.

The Aspirations of Private Engagement and "Health-Sector Envy"

To inform decisionmaking on the constituency model during the transition from the FTI to the GPE, a working group was delegated the task of producing suggestions for the board composition, which was presented at a board meeting in 2010. As stated in the meeting document: "The working group was informed by a number of discussions and interviews with different FTI stakeholders as well as actors working with other global (mainly health) initiatives" (GPE, 2010, p. 1); also at that meeting, a consultancy report was presented, entitled *Strengths and Weaknesses in the Governance of Selected Global Health Initiatives* (Stenson, 2010).

Experiences from the health sector, therefore, played a fundamental role in informing how the GPE board would be constituted. While these suggestions, informed in large part by experience with the Global Fund to Fight AIDS, Tuberculosis, and Malaria and GAVI: The Vaccine Alliance, covered several aspects of successful governance and included rationales for including the private sector. Indicated in the suggestions was an eagerness to include the private sector as potential donors because they "also represent a relatively unrestricted source of funding for special projects within FTI" (GPE, 2010, p. 10). Although a model that included private-sector actors as donors did not come to fruition, the early ideals around private financing were evident.

Interviewees, moreover, note the attempt to map the health-sector experiences in private financing onto the GPE. As one respondent described, the actors within the private-sector/foundation constituency had been often compared to health, where "they kept looking at what happened in health and saying 'Well, how do we get this constituency to be more nontraditional donors, actually to put money into GPE?'" (personal communication, private sector/foundation, January 31, 2014). Another interviewee stated simply that within the FTI/GPE, "there has always been a little bit of health-sector envy" (personal communication, Secretariat, September 24, 2014). And yet, "[y]ou don't have foundations in the education sector the size of the foundations in health . . . We are not the health sector" (personal communication, private sector/foundation, January 31, 2014). Moreover, there are far more large-scale MSP partnerships focusing on health-related issues—including, for example, the Global Fund, the Global Alliance for Improved Nutrition (GAIN), GAVI, the International Health Partnership, and the Roll Back Malaria Partnership—that include major representation of the private sector in both policymaking and financing (Bezanson & Isenman, 2012). Such private participation is simply not of the same size, type, or level of engagement in education. The prevalent discourse of the GPE includes taken-for-granted expectations that private actors will function similarly to those within multistakeholder partnerships in the health sector. But according to respondents, despite assumed parallels between the two sectors, private financing to GPE is considered unrealistic.

The Reality of Private Engagement: Conflicts in Goals and Mandates

However, as shown in meeting documents, and from the perspective of interviewees, the GPE Secretariat continues to view the private-sector/foundation constituency in an aspirational way, in the hope that its members might contribute to the GPE Fund. For instance, at a board meeting, the Secretariat introduced a broad strategy for the GPE's future replenishment campaign, which included: "Central to the strategy for a successful replenishment was the need to focus on financing from four core target groups, namely traditional donors, developing country partners, emerging donors and *the private sector, including private foundations*" (GPE, 2013b, p. 7; emphasis mine). Interviewees concur that the Secretariat seemed to be pushing for private-sector contributions to the GPE Fund, framing the private sector as an important financial source.

But the following statements made in interviews with board members indicate an improbability that the GPE Fund will ever receive substantial contributions from the private sector: "There's been some fairly unsophisticated thinking on the part of the Secretariat, [that] the private sector would . . . make financial contributions to the GPE Fund. By the way, that's incredibly unrealistic" (personal communication, CSO, January 13, 2014); "I struggle to see them putting money into either the core cost of the Secretariat or the big pot of money that is the GPE Fund" (personal communication, private sector/foundation, February 3, 2014); "I don't think there is any chance that's going to happen" (personal communication, private sector/foundation, January 21, 2014); "The private sector, these companies nor foundations, nobody is about to cut the check and put money into the GPE Fund. . . . It's a nice thing to talk about, but it's simply not going to happen" (personal communication, private sector/foundation, February 4, 2014).

As a respondent described, the nature of private funding is a "moving target" (personal communication, UN/multilateral agency, April 4, 2014). At this time, four foundations have made funding commitments to GPE, but these total a tiny fraction of the total funding—less than 0.25 percent (GPE, 2018b). No private companies have yet to make funding commitments, and interviewees have expressed doubt that this will change. Media commenters, following a GPE funding replenishment conference, stated that "GPE has failed yet again to convince businesses to pledge money to the fund" (Ravelo & Jones, 2014).

This limited degree of private-sector financial support is rooted in part in the apparent priorities of the private sector, in particular the importance of tracking investments. Companies "are not funding initiatives like this," but instead are seen to "invest in solutions and . . . expect returns on things and want to see the results" (personal communication, private sector/foundation, January 21, 2014). But another respondent stated, "It's hard for a foundation to say, I'm going to give a dollar into a pooled fund, unless it's for symbolic reasons, because you're accountable to your board, and particularly with the new wave of foundations, they are in it for very specific, trackable outcomes" (personal communication, private sector/foundation, January 31, 2014). A mismatch is therefore evident between the aspirations and the reality concerning private contributions to the GPE Fund. In light of this, the attempts to parallel experiences with the health sector, where large pooled contributions are commonly made from the private sector, are simply unrealistic. And this incongruity between what is desired of the private-sector/foundation constituency members and how they are in fact willing to function as partners within the GPE creates an ambiguous situation.

Several interviewees expressed that the role of the private-sector/foundation seat had always lacked clarity. As early as 2011, the constituency felt the need to better define its role within the context of the GPE board and as nonfunders. At the Copenhagen Pledging Conference in November 2011, a constituency member made a "Statement from Private Sector and Private Foundations," which began with the following: "I represent one of the board's newest and most diverse constituencies: private sector and private foundations. We don't give funds directly to the GPE Fund, so you may be wondering why we're here" (GPE, 2011, p. 1). The statement indicates that relatively early in the restructured board, the private-sector/foundation constituency felt the need to clarify its involvement in the GPE and to draw attention to its nonmonetary contributions.

Yet the lack of clarity persists, and private-sector/foundation board members feel that they are continually questioning their role within the GPE: "What is the rationale for involving the private sector in this in the first place, and what is it that the GPE as a partnership and the Secretariat want from the private sector? You know, conversely, what does the private sector feel are the benefits and values from being involved? I don't think any of this has ever been fleshed out" (personal communication, private sector/foundation, January 21, 2014). Constituency members have seen themselves as needing to answer the questions: "Why are you contributing? Why are you at the table?" Therefore, they are "constantly having to explain what the value added is . . ." (personal communication, private sector/foundation, January 31, 2014). Interviewees described the constituency members as "frustrated" as they attempted to "find out ways to keep the business side interested" (personal communication, CSO, March 3, 2015). Private actors who see themselves as able to offer ideas and "solutions" to educational problems have not been substantively supported within the GPE to take on this role. As another respondent summarized: "internally, and also with the GPE Secretariat, they have yet to figure out how to best utilize the [private sector/foundation] constituency as a resource" (personal communication, private sector/foundation, February 4, 2014).

Moreover, citing this lack of clarity, respondents described a limited engagement in GPE on the part of the private-sector/foundation members: "I think that the private sector has not seen the benefit of engaging the GPE, why would they do that, what's in it for them?" (personal communication, private sector/foundation, February 21, 2014). Similarly, another interviewee expressed that "the GPE still struggles so much to get the private sector as fully engaged as it would like" (personal communication, Secretariat, September 14, 2014).

A further concern within the private-sector/foundation constituency, likely linked to the lack of clarity as to its role, is what some have described as a considerable conflict between the foundations and companies, as well as the problematic nature of their sharing of a board seat. Described as "strange bedfellows" and "different organizational animals," interviewees plainly see a difference between the two types of constituency members: "just a totally different kettle of fish." As one interviewee elaborated: "Unfortunately private foundations and the private sector [companies] in this, they come from two completely different angles. The private sector is very much interested in okay, how are we going to increase our profit margin? For even if it's a corporate social responsibility arm, they're not there because they're just purely interested in education . . ." (personal communication, private sector/foundation, February 4, 2014). Companies are described as focused on "profit as bottom-line, versus [foundations,] where giving away is the bottom line," (personal communication, private sector/foundation, January 31, 2014), and that the constituency is "not a consolidated group, and they have very, very different interests" (personal communication, Secretariat, August 20, 2014). As a result of such divergent objectives, there has been some mistrust and tension within the constituency in the past.

As one interviewee pointed out, "[Y]ou can already see that there was both tension and a desire for autonomy of those two combined constituencies, because they are quite different" (personal communication, CSO, January 13, 2014). As an example, one issue cited as having a strong potential for tension concerns the recent rise in low-cost private schools in recipient countries, where some private-sector/foundation members would like to see more engagement with the private sector at the country level, and others describe GPE support to low-cost private schools as deeply problematic.

Discussions have continued up to the present day, and board proposals put forward, all seeking to split the constituency seat between the companies and foundations. As one interviewee stated: "From [the foundation] perspective . . . well that's fabulous, please have your own seat and take the rest of your private-sector companies with you" (personal communication, private sector/foundation, February 4, 2014). Yet, the private-sector/foundation constituency continues to hold only a single seat on the board. One reason cited was the continued desire to keep the board at a manageable size. Other reasons, however, highlighted the ambiguity around the private sector/foundation's role within the GPE. For instance, some board members expressed dissatisfaction with expanding the role of the private sector/foundation without committing resources to the GPE Fund. For example: "I'm not sure that the private sector deserves its own seat on the board, per se. It's a player, but simply in terms of direct contributions to the mission of the GPE, its contributions continue to be very modest. They haven't had any financial contributions to GPE, and they haven't necessarily mobilized a huge amount of support for education to this day. . . . It's not a bad thing that they have a more modest representation on the board" (personal communication, CSO, January 13, 2014). In fact, some interviewees described the private sector/foundation as being too involved as decisionmakers rather than occupying the roles they ought to play as funders: "[T]he private sector is hugely important in education, but they should participate through making contributions to the GPE Fund, basically . . . they should not be involved in setting the agenda for education on the ground" (personal communication, CSO, March 3, 2014).

Another significant reason cited for the rejection of the proposal for separate board seats was the fact that the private sector/foundation had yet to influence any particular policy directions within the GPE: "We hadn't really made an impact as a joint constituency because we were so busy looking at each other and being suspicious, and what does that mean, and why are these people here, and . . . not really being as engaged and energized and mobilized as a constituency to really make an impact on the GPE. It was almost like we haven't even justified our individual seat, so why would we need two seats?" (personal communication, private sector/foundation, February 21, 2014). Another interviewee explained that the members of the constituency "function on paper but they really didn't come together as a very meaningful entity" (personal communication, Secretariat, September 24, 2014). The lack of engagement, driven by the incongruence between aims and interconstituency distrust, has led to few achievements as a constituency.

The Discourse of Private Actors in Global Partnership for Education

The GPE case highlights the complexity of private participation and private authority. Private-sector members—including both companies and foundations—are included as key stakeholders in GPE, particularly in its governance as members of its board of directors. Since the early days of the restructuring from the FTI, the role of the private partners within the GPE's governance has been poorly clarified. Also problematic has been the internal conflict between foundations and companies, who see themselves as distinct actors who aim to serve different purposes, in contrast to other stakeholders that deem it appropriate for foundations and companies to sit together on the board. Despite a desire to serve a policymaking function within the partnership, with a seat at the table, private actors are relatively disengaged.

This disengagement and lack of clarification are rooted in an aspirational discourse that assumes that private actors would serve a financing function to the GPE Fund, based largely on inaccurate parallels made between the health and education sectors. This borrowing from health-sector experiences has fed a particularly positive, yet arguably inaccurate, discourse relating to the private sector. According to its most recent charter, the GPE (2018a, p. 9) frames the roles of private actors as those who can "[b]ring technical expertise, voice, innovation, networks and experience to address the complex challenges of delivering education." As stated on the GPE website (2018c):

> GPE aims to improve equitable access to education, better learning outcomes and support more efficient education systems in partnership with the business community as follows:
> - Leverage the private sector's technical expertise and resources
> - Tap into the advocacy power of the business community to increase understanding of, and support for, the work of GPE at global and national levels
> - Deepen the business community's involvement in education planning and policy dialogue at national and global levels
> - Secure new and additional financing for GPE from companies and private organizations

The last of these bullets, according to respondents, guides much of the GPE's engagement with private actors, where the private sector is viewed predominantly as a source of funds. However, it is the discourse relating to "technical expertise," "innovation," and "advocacy power" that arguably drives the perceived legitimacy of private actors, which are afforded a certain degree of voice on the GPE board, given a particular framing of their capacities. Private-sector entities hold the potential for policy influence by virtue of their presence and being embraced by the Secretariat and other stakeholders.

This legitimacy has been granted despite the fact that companies and foundations have not been deeply engaged with GPE in most respects. According to respondents, little incentive exists for private actors to truly participate in GPE, beyond board membership. In this sense, the GPE arguably presents an in-practice case of the private sector's potential to exercise an exit option: disengagement because the partnership needs the private sector more than the foundations or companies need the partnership. Their participation shows that they have the power to exit, or to be relatively disengaged if they wish.

As will be discussed in further detail in the concluding chapter of this book, the GPE case demonstrates a case of productive power, where the partnership and its stakeholders accept an aspirational discursive framing of private actors that feeds a desire for increased private engagement. Meanwhile, in reality, private actors have shown little proof that this discourse reflects reality, and they hold the power to decide when and if to engage, and in what capacity.

CONCLUSION

The goal of this chapter has been twofold: to show how power operates through the GPE as, first, structural power through the reproduction of hierarchies; and second, productive power through the diffusion of discourse relating to the private sector. Through detailing the ways in which northern actors retain power in the partnership and the nuanced and aspirational way that the private sector has been framed relative to its actual engagement, this chapter contributes to the wider aim of this book: to offer a more complex understanding of the multifaceted nature of the relationships within partnership-based arrangements in education. As argued by Barnett and Duvall (2005a): "Understanding power in this way makes it much more difficult to approach global governance purely in terms of cooperation, coordination, consensus, and/or normative progress; governance is also a matter of institutional or systemic bias, privilege, and unequal constraints on action" (p. 17). As educational partnerships proliferate globally, the case of the GPE presents an exemplar of how to understand the degree to which collaborative relationships connote equity and the need to identify who truly wields power within them.

In the next chapter, I expose the similar ways in which power hierarchies reinscribe within another partnership-based organization: the ECW. Then I revisit GPE in the concluding chapter in a discussion and comparison with the ECW, and I also show how a network lens helps to understand both.

NOTES

1. Although the analysis of GPE has been supported by key informant interviews conducted in 2014 and 2015, in order to update and confirm that the findings herein remain relevant, brief follow-up interviews with several respondents were conducted in 2017 and 2018.

2. The Grant Agent was previously termed a *supervising entity*.

CHAPTER 5

The Challenges of Partnering for Aid to Education in Emergencies

The Case of the Education Cannot Wait Fund

Contexts of conflict, fragility, and emergency present particular challenges for educational aid. The traditional aid architecture has been near-universally deemed not fit for purpose when it comes to contexts of crisis. Experts and organizations such as the Inter-Agency Network for Education in Emergencies (INEE) have made calls for many years to revisit aid policy in light of shortcomings to the typical architecture, which often includes requirements that governments of conflict-affected and fragile contexts cannot meet. And although the international community has elevated the issue of education in emergencies to become a policy priority in more recent years, with some organizations even changing their mandate and funding mechanisms (Menashy & Dryden-Peterson, 2015), humanitarian aid has remained "chronically underfunded" (GPE, 2015, p. 1), inadequate to reach those considered most vulnerable in settings of crisis and "poorly aligned with real world imperatives" (ODI, 2016, p. 7).

Moreover, traditional aid policy focuses largely on the need for countries to display good performance and well-established planning to receive loans, requiring a degree of stability that is not possible in contexts of emergency. Some funding platforms include parameters that disqualify countries facing emergencies from applying for loans. For example, the Global Partnership for Education (GPE) only funds low-income countries, leaving out middle-income states who host refugees. In addition, most international financing to education is state based, presenting logistical challenges to funding education for migrant populations who cross borders. Critics, moreover, widely consider aid distribution far too bureaucratic, slow, and inflexible to respond to sudden emergencies, citing the need for a rapid and more agile response mechanism. Also, aid in the contexts of crisis and conflict typically supports short-term, immediate interventions, neglecting the need for long-term, systemic solutions (Dryden-Peterson, 2017; GPE, 2015).

Finally, over a decade after the establishment of the Millennium Development Goals (MDGs), while many countries made significant progress in achieving universal education, children living in contexts of fragility and crisis continued to lack access to quality education. As a donor representative explained: "[T]hose bottom performers hadn't improved substantially or were still at the bottom; it really said something about the ineffectual approaches to these fragile contexts" (personal communication, bilateral donor, July 8, 2016).

The Education Cannot Wait Fund (ECW) was established to address these significant and longstanding constraints to providing adequate aid to education in contexts of crisis. As a multistakeholder (MSP) global pooled fund comprising the resources of a range of partners, based on principles of collaboration, coordination, and partnership in governance, as well as participatory processes at the country level, ECW reflects the trend toward partnership in global education. As this chapter will detail, despite its genuine intentions, ECW retains a familiar power structure reminiscent of the traditional aid architecture, reflecting structural power where a few selective actors, predominantly from the Global North, hold positions of power. ECW, moreover, presents a case of productive power in which the private sector has been harnessed to play roles in which they wield legitimate authority and influence based on an aspirational discourse, even without committing resources.

THE HISTORY AND MANDATE OF
THE EDUCATION CANNOT WAIT FUND

For several years, agencies that focus, either solely or tangentially, on education in emergencies had floated and discussed ideas for a stand-alone funding mechanism targeting education in emergencies. Many actors working in the education in emergencies sector believed that simply revising the policies or operations of existing agencies would not sufficiently address the many shortcomings of traditional aid. Beyond these criticisms, a few additional factors converged around the mid-2010s, which interview respondents view as catalysts for the establishment of ECW. The Syrian refugee crisis had come to the forefront of humanitarian aid discussions, and in particular the global community's limited means to support the education of Syrian children displaced in neighboring countries. The lead-up consultations to the 2015 establishment of the Sustainable Development Goals (SDGs) also allowed a convergence of voices for the SDGs to better address education in humanitarian contexts than the MDGs had done.

By the mid-2010s, several parallel discussions were underway, voicing the need for a new global fund with a single mandate to support education in contexts of crisis. Interview respondents cited 2015 as pivotal, with the GPE convening discussions on the possibility of a new platform and producing a March 2015 issues paper entitled *A Platform for Education in Crisis and Conflict*, which outlined areas that could be targeted by a new fund, basic principles that might inform the decision to initiate a new platform, and some of the potential risks involved (GPE, 2015). That year also saw the formation of working groups on the potential establishment of a new fund, including representatives from United Nations (UN) agencies, nongovernmental organizations (NGOs), bilateral donors, multilateral agencies, businesses, consultants, and, most notably, the office of the UN Special Envoy for Global Education, Gordon Brown. Widely seen as the single most pivotal player in the establishment of ECW, Brown was described as "leading the charge" (personal communication, bilateral donor, July 8, 2016), having "spearheaded" ECW (personal communication, UN/multilateral agency, February 6, 2017). ECW was largely built off a May 2016 Overseas Development Institute (ODI) report entitled *Education Cannot Wait: Proposing a Fund for Education in Emergencies*, which was commissioned by UNICEF on behalf of several agencies, including the UN Special Envoy for Education, governments, other UN branches, foundations, NGOs, Global Business Coalition for Education (GBC-E), GPE, INEE, and the World Bank, and was financed by the United Kingdom's Department for International Development (DfID), the government of Norway, and the United States Agency for International Development (USAID). The Boston Consulting Group (BCG) was also commissioned to conduct a needs analysis and offer recommendations on the design, operating model, and results framework of ECW (BCG, 2016, 2017).

Additionally, a global consultation on education in emergencies and protracted crisis, conducted by INEE, in part informed the ODI report. The INEE report of findings, released in March 2016, detailed "areas of consensus, concern, and recommendation pertaining to questions posed on the conceptual framework, priority functions, and scale of the proposed 'Common Platform' for education in emergencies and protracted crises" based on interviews and feedback from over 500 experts and practitioners from the field of education in emergencies, including representatives from state- and nonstate-sector global organizations, as well as "teachers, students, and members from crisis affected countries" (INEE, 2016, p. 1). This INEE report, its history, and its impact on the ODI report (and, by extension, ECW) will be discussed later in this chapter.

The ODI report laid out a clear rationale for ECW, explaining the ways in which the traditional aid architecture effectively failed those living in contexts of crisis and emergency. In it, ECW was proposed as innovative and unique, a way to "transform the global education sectors" (ODI, 2016, p. 10). It also cited the "fault lines" highlighted by the Syria crisis, as well as the newly established SDGs, as "a new window of opportunity" focusing increased worldwide attention on education in emergency contexts (p. 11). The report portrayed ECW as a way to bridge the divide between humanitarian and development aid through a rapid-response financing mechanism, while also inspiring increased political commitment, joint planning and response, funding generation and distribution, capacity building, and improving accountability systems (p. 15). The report also included proposals for governance and possible funding mechanisms.

ECW was officially launched in May 2016 at the World Humanitarian Summit in Istanbul, representing the culmination of several years of mobilization toward a global fund targeted specifically to education in emergency contexts. As stated in its 2018 strategic plan, the organization seeks to "transform the aid system" with a new approach to educational aid that responds to the need for more flexible and rapid financing of education in settings of emergency; ECW is "the only financing mechanism specifically focused on the dual mission of speedy education responses in emergencies, as well as durable efficiency and quality of education for the long run" (ECW, 2018d, p. 8). Financing education takes on a new level of urgency in contexts of crisis, where existing aid mechanisms are viewed as unable to respond in a timely and flexible way.

The funding modalities include a "First Emergency Response" investment window to address immediate educational needs in contexts of sudden crisis, as well as a "Multi-Year Resilience" investment window to offer long-term support. ECW proposes that the multiyear programs allow humanitarian and development actors to collaborate in supporting education, particularly in contexts of protracted crises (ECW, 2018b). Its "Acceleration Facility" funds research and data collection. At this time, ECW has invested $134.5 million toward education in 19 countries affected by crisis.

ECW's governance includes a High-Level Steering Group (HLSG), composed of 18 principal members (17 of which are voting members), representing constituencies including bilateral donors, beneficiary-country governments, the private sector, foundations, and civil society organizations (CSOs), as well as from UNICEF, UNHCR, UNESCO, INEE, GPE, and the UN Special Envoy for Global Education (ECW, 2018c). HLSG members' tasks include resource mobilization, deciding on ECW strategic directions and policy, and approving financing arrangements and funding for multiyear grants (ECW, 2018c, pp. 5–6). The Executive Committee is an operational oversight body, also including 18 members, approving smaller grants and annual budgets, and overseeing administrative operations (ECW, 2018a). An Independent Proposal Review Panel, composed of experts from the field, assists in the decisions of the HLSG through technical reviews and recommendations on grant proposals (ECW, 2018b). A Secretariat hosted by UNICEF provides administrative support to the fund and is housed within UNICEF headquarters in New York, led by Director Yasmin Sharif. UNICEF is also the ECW's funds custodian, managing all contracts and disbursing resources (ECW, 2018a, 2018b).

ECW country-level processes involve "bringing together existing leadership and coordination groups as needed to make proposals and decisions regarding Platform support appropriate to the crisis" (ODI, 2016, p. 18). In cases of a First Response Window, distribution involves small, initial funds to address immediate concerns following a crisis, or to respond to project proposals forwarded by organizations already preaccredited by ECW's donors through a grant proposal process (ECW, 2018b). In First Response Window programs, ECW works within countries alongside a coordinating entity (e.g., an education cluster or refugee coordination group) to determine priorities and direct resources directly to preaccredited implementing agencies. In the case of a Multi-Year Window, in order to support longer-term education programs (3 to 5 years), ECW works through a range of grantees, including UN agencies and international and national NGOs (ECW, 2018a, 2018b).

As overarching aims, ECW promotes collaboration and coordination, and "seeks to remove barriers preventing humanitarian and development actors, governments, NGOs and the private sector from combining efforts to address growing and urgent education needs in emergencies and protracted crises" (ECW, 2018d, p. 8). ECW's partnership structure promotes a "joint-programming approach" and "close collaboration amongst all actors" to produce "collective effectiveness and better outcomes" (ECW, 2018d, p. 8). A key aspect of ECW is its public–private structure, and as will be discussed later in this chapter, an explicit goal of ECW is attracting new sources of financing, with a strong focus on the private sector. As this chapter details, ECW holds as a core principle "national ownership" (ECW, 2018d, p. 14), where ECW beneficiaries and people affected by crises "are actively involved in designing and implementing the response . . . increasing national ownership" (ECW, 2018d, p. 10). Such organizational principles reflect a wider development agenda shift toward increased southern community participation and voices in decisionmaking.

POWER DYNAMICS IN EDUCATION CANNOT WAIT

Power in Education Cannot Wait Governance

Although the idea of a global fund targeting education in emergencies had been suggested by many actors for several years, the design of ECW occurred at a relatively rapid pace, with preliminary discussions happening in early 2015 and the official launch of the fund in May 2016. Those with initial input into the ECW design and mandate represented UN agencies, multilateral and bilateral donors, the Special Envoy's Office, and private-sector actors, which collaborated to produce the abovementioned ODI report. Brown and other policy high-level actors, therefore, were central to the establishment of the fund. Yet, after an initial draft of the ODI report, criticisms were raised that ECW would lack legitimacy without a more inclusive foundation, and so the INEE was asked to conduct a wide consultation on the development of ECW. The consultation was conducted between January and March 2016, in multiple languages, and sought to elicit feedback on an early draft of the ODI report that included the views of over 500 practitioners, policymakers, UN agencies, civil society groups, national and local NGOs, and educators from around the world. The respondents widely viewed this INEE consultation as providing ECW with a more solid foundation, but as an interviewee involved in the consultation process explained:

> The idea was a little bit token. . . . To me it seemed like it was almost an afterthought of getting input from the practitioners in the field, the people actually working in education in emergencies programs, not just high-level policymakers and donors [who] managed to sideline some of the important players and voices that aren't heads of state or the movers and shakers in the finance world. (personal communication, independent observer, October 4, 2018)

The views expressed in the INEE consultations highlighted some major concerns about ECW that several actors saw as significant and necessary to address. Most respondents agreed about the necessity of a new fund and the need to rethink the financing of education in emergencies. Yet questions were raised concerning issues of potential duplication of existing mechanisms, such as securing financing that would not displace other funding to education, along with concerns relating to accountability, transparency, and participation. The INEE consultation, for instance, stated that the draft ODI report "does not make clear what role different actors can play and how they can interact with and contribute to the decision-making processes of the platform, from civil society to local and national NGOs, local education groups, country-level education clusters, local and national governments, the business community, international NGOs, UN agencies, GPE, INEE, etc. . . . Many respondents specifically requested building a clear mechanism for constituency engagement and participation, including people affected by emergencies" (INEE, 2016, p. 4).

While ECW indeed solicited input beyond high-level policy and government actor viewpoints, including practitioners at the country level and local actors, from the perspectives of some respondents the INEE consultation was an afterthought and tokenized particular participants. Also, as will be discussed later in this chapter, concerns remain relating to the participation of communities, local actors, and people affected by emergency.

Interview respondents also criticized the governance of ECW as exclusive and nonparticipatory. The HLSG was described as selective and limited to a small group of those considered leaders in the education and development arenas. And, as respondents described, ECW continues to be dominated by particular organizations, while some actors have felt excluded from the process. For instance, UNICEF has been deeply involved with ECW in the past both with design and as host. Meanwhile, UNESCO has not, and as a respondent lamented, it often only received invitations to meetings and consultations at the very last minute. Further, "civil society organizations engaged in education in emergencies are extremely frustrated. They haven't been able to engage here at all" (personal communication, UN/multilateral agency, February 6, 2017), despite the INEE consultation stressing the importance of civil society engagement.

By some accounts, ECW governance is characterized by favoritism, including primarily those with established and positive relationships with Gordon Brown's office. For instance, representatives from the GBC-E have been involved since the early days of the fund, participating in initial discussions, meetings, consultations, and now sitting on its HLSG. Yet, as will be discussed in more detail later in this chapter, GBC-E was founded and led by Gordon Brown's wife, Sarah.

Also reflecting a degree of favoritism, beneficiary-country voice has been, and continues to be, represented by those with established and positive relationships with Gordon Brown. As a respondent explains, beneficiary-country representatives in ECW governance "largely were individuals that were friendly to the [fund]. And Gordon Brown identified them . . . there was no real process of consultation. It just boiled down to Gordon Brown and the [ECW] Secretariat identifying some champion countries who could be on the board" (personal communication, UN/multilateral agency, September 20, 2018).

When asked if ECW governance includes a range of stakeholder voices and if the processes appear participatory and equitable, a respondent replied: "They keep going on about transparency, but it's not really what's happening . . . there was never any proper system to who was included and who wasn't" (personal communication, UN/multilateral agency, February 6, 2017). When asked about beneficiary-country engagement in ECW governance, a respondent replied: "They're not well represented in the governance structures" (personal communication, bilateral donor, July 8, 2018). Another respondent explained that "someone like Gordon Brown is thinking much more about high-level policy . . . I mean, if you look at the executive committee of ECW, it's those policy-level [people]. Those people aren't thinking about local voices" (personal communication, independent observer, October 4, 2018). ECW governance appears to be more exclusive than inclusive and participatory, reflecting preferences rather than open and transparent selection processes: "[W]hether they've actually done it [governance] in a systematic or transparent way that is democratic and really gives voice to certain participants, is debatable" (personal communication, UN/multilateral agency, September 20, 2018).

The Power of UNICEF

Respondents repeatedly identified UNICEF as a core player in ECW from its earliest establishment until the present, as its host and funds custodian.

UNICEF is officially hosting ECW during its incubation for the initial start-up. The decision to house the fund at UNICEF was informed by an external hosting review conducted by the consulting group Mokoro Ltd., which systematically compared a shortlist of various organizations that could feasibly serve as host, including UNICEF, GPE, the Multi-Partner Trust Fund Office of the United Nations Development Programme (UNDP), the United Nations Office for Project Services, and the World Bank. Although the review recommended that UNICEF remain as host for the duration of the 2018–2021 strategy, the consulting group cautioned that UNICEF's hosting should not preclude other agencies from acting as host in the future (Mokoro, 2018).

UNICEF's main competition for host, according to interview respondents, has been the GPE. Some stakeholders viewed GPE as having the infrastructure and expertise already in place to manage and distribute funds, as well as a newly developed policy on fragile states: "My general position then, and remains the same now, is that it would have been better for it to have set within GPE" (personal communication, UN/multilateral agency, September 20, 2018). As will be discussed later, some proponents of GPE hosting questioned the establishment of ECW as a separate fund that would then feasibly duplicate or compete with GPE's financing.

The decision to host ECW within UNICEF rather than GPE came down to a few factors. First, GPE was viewed as lacking the mechanisms to ensure that funds would be disbursed at a rapid speed and also without established relationships to humanitarian actors and the security clearance for its staff to work immediately in emergency response. Most important, however, GPE's own hosting situation has been in flux for many years, as described in Chapter 4. Given that some stakeholders saw GPE as potentially breaking from its World Bank relationship sometime in the future, hosting ECW in an uncertain environment would not be sensible.

Yet some major critiques of UNICEF as host have been raised, primarily relating to potential conflicts of interest. As the hosting review report explains, "[D]ependence on UNICEF for access carries risks of perceptions of conflict of interest which need mitigation" (Mokoro, 2018, p. 9).

The review cited three main areas in which conflict of interest is likely to be an issue:

a) Fundraising: ECW and a host may, in effect, be competing for funds from the same sources.
b) Grant allocation: There is an obvious potential conflict of interest if an organization involved in allocating grants is itself a potential recipient.
c) Accountability for grant utilization: Similarly, there is a potential conflict of interest if a host seems to be involved in the monitoring and evaluation of its own grant utilization. Moreover, part of

ECW's remit (Core Function 5) is to "improve accountability by developing and sharing knowledge . . . of what works and what does not." This could involve (constructive) criticism of a host's performance in [education in emergencies], whether or not ECW funds were involved. (Mokoro, 2018, p. 12)

Respondents echoed these criticisms, worrying about a situation where "funds are going from UNICEF to UNICEF" (personal communication, bilateral donor, October 2, 2018). An NGO respondent expressed some doubt about the validity of the hosting arrangement: "I think there's still a lot of questions around the platform itself and how funds will get distributed and why UNICEF was selected to be the holder of the funds . . . how much overhead is UNICEF going to take out of the fund?" (personal communication, NGO, July 6, 2016). Others voiced concerns that "the influence of UNICEF is kind of beyond what it should be . . . the fact is that UNICEF is still one of the biggest implementers in both the humanitarian response to education crisis" (personal communication, UN/multilateral agency, September 2, 2018).

Ultimately, the hosting review recommended that UNICEF remain as host for the incubation period of the fund, noting, "It is therefore important to make all efforts to mitigate conflict of interest at UNICEF, not least because of its ongoing role as the host during incubation. Genuine and transparent autonomy of the Secretariat is a key factor in mitigating conflict of interest and perceptions of conflict of interest" (Mokoro, 2018, p. 12). It also recommended that financial hosting should be transferred to another multidonor trust fund. And, according to respondent reports, the HLSG in 2018 agreed that UNICEF's incubation period will continue until 2021. Yet critics noted UNICEF's outsize influence and potential to receive disproportionate benefits from its hosting of ECW. The dominance of this single organization within ECW is in turn viewed as having shut out others, with UNICEF viewed as the "big player" (personal communication, UN/multilateral agency, July 11, 2016). Another respondent described UNICEF's ostensibly temporary hosting as "a crazy decision" (personal communication, UN/multilateral agency, September 20, 2018).

Hosting ECW within UNICEF, moreover, raised concerns about duplication and poor coordination between partnership-based funding mechanisms, where ECW might compete directly with other MSPs (most notably GPE) for donor funds. In 2015, the GPE issues paper warned that a new fund for education in crisis and conflict could risk "further fragmentation of the sector if the new platform is not established in such a manner as to leverage greater coordination, harmonization, and alignment across existing donors in the sector" (GPE, 2015, p. 14). According to ECW's strategic plan, the fund indeed places coordination as central to its efforts: "Traditionally, the humanitarian and development sectors have suffered from a fragmented system that tends to create silos, disjointedness, and inefficiencies . . . ECW was created to remove barriers preventing humanitarian and development actors, governments, NGOs and the private sector from combining efforts to address growing and urgent education needs in emergencies and protracted crises" (ECW, 2018, p. 8).

Yet respondents expressed the opinion that ECW has not adequately addressed risks of fragmentation. One respondent stated: "I think there's a kind of competition for who rules, so I think it's also in the interest of Gordon Brown to have a separate mechanism" (personal communication, UN/multilateral agency, September 20, 2018). Another put it more bluntly: "It's ruthless turf war that goes on. It's not about the objectives and aims. It's about knocking certain organizations out of the way in order to gain" (personal communication, UN/multilateral agency, February 6, 2017). In direct contrast to the goals of coordination and harmonization, respondents describe ECW as exacerbating a competitive aid environment in which certain individuals and organizations achieve success at the expense of others.

Power Dynamics in Country-Level Operations

Respondents also noted the impact of poor coordination on country-level, local actors, creating confusion and competing messages; one of them stated: "I think the countries are really struggling because they are being approached by different funders with different sort of, 'We can provide you with this and our requirements in the education-sector plan.' Then Education Cannot Wait comes in, and they say, 'We can provide you this' and so everybody's banging, knocking on the door . . . The impression that I have is that they [beneficiary countries] get very confused" (personal communication, bilateral donor, October 2, 2018).

The ECW mandate envisions its country-level activities as aligning with INEE's minimum standards and global mandates relating to participation of recipients, making clear that not only must recipient governments be engaged in decisionmaking on aid, but local NGOs and members of affected communities must as well. According to the INEE minimum standards handbook (2010, p. 22), one of the "foundational standards" of good practice in emergency contexts is community participation, where "[c]ommunity members participate actively, transparently and without discrimination in analysis, planning, design, implementation, monitoring and evaluation of education responses." It continues:

> Effective emergency education response is based on active community participation—processes and activities that empower people to take part in decision-making processes and take action on education issues. Community involvement and ownership enhance accountability, strengthen the mobilisation of local resources and support the maintenance of education services in the long

term. Participation facilitates the identification of education issues particular to the local context and ways to address them. . . . . Community participation should include capacity building for community members and build upon education activities already being carried out. The participation of children and youth, who can contribute to community resilience and recovery, is very important. (p. 20)

In accordance with this, ECW includes as a component of its Principles and Core Functions "country ownership" (ECW, 2018d, p. 14) and "promotes the localization agenda":

ECWs flexible funding and direct execution modalities allow it to be context-specific and invest in a wide range of partners, including governments, UN agencies, [and] international and local NGOs. ECW proactively invests in local and national responders . . . advancing the "aid localization agenda". . . . Through its localization approach, ECW also ensures affected people and local stakeholders are actively involved in designing and implementing the response, empowering local capacities, supporting better and more sustainable education outcomes and increasing national ownership. (p. 10)

Yet all respondents interviewed based on their engagement in ECW voiced the opinion that local participation, including both governments and communities, has been limited at best, and that within beneficiary countries, engagement continues to be northern dominant, where high-level policy and donor actors are primarily driving ECW processes. Limited local engagement affects some core ECW goals, particularly related to capacity building and community participation.

Capacity building was cited as a key ECW need identified by the INEE consultation, where a range of stakeholders noted that an early draft of the ODI report did not treat this with enough emphasis. Although ECW strategy now includes as a core goal to strengthen the capacity of those leading education efforts, including local actors and governments (see ECW, 2018d), respondents explained that ECW has yet to solidly implement capacity building within their recipient countries, voicing concerns "around the need to ensure local ownership and ensure the building of government capacity," and that capacity building has been "downplayed" (personal communication, NGO, June 7, 2017).

Beyond the building of capacity within beneficiary countries, it appears that ECW has not adequately engaged with governments, often failing to consult with ministries of education. ECW country-level interactions with local actors were characterized by respondents as "limited," or engaging in "little dialogue" with governments. ECW's earliest initial operations were described as taking a "standard humanitarian approach," free from government coordination, or "coming in a helicopter or parachuting in . . . you could say 'the UN system approach'. And then creating a program, but with a very limited dialogue with other actors and especially with government and local communities" (personal communication, bilateral donor, October 2, 2018). This approach was critiqued ("it couldn't fly") and the country-level operations were revised to explicitly stress the need for dialogue with local government bodies and communities. But beyond the on-paper proposal, respondents noted that inadequate government coordination remains. In some cases, proposed ECW funding was described as having no input from local government actors. As one in-country respondent put it, the ECW process "[c]ompletely bypassed the ministry. And it really frightened me" (personal communication, independent observer, December 18, 2018).

Although ECW strategy clearly aligns with INEE minimum standards relating to local community participation and the need for local dialogue in the design and implementation of funded activities, respondents noted that this rhetoric has not adequately manifested in reality: "[I]n the case of Education Cannot Wait, there is, on paper, you have participation of partner counties. But the reality is that there isn't" (personal communication, bilateral donor, October 2, 2018). Others note that "what is laid out is that it is going to very much field-driven. It's going to respond to needs on the ground. Local actors are going to be equal to big UN agencies when it comes to receiving funds. . . . It looks beautiful and very right . . . on paper" (personal communication, UN/multilateral agency, February 6, 2017). Another respondent noted widespread concerns, with "people saying, 'No, there needs to be voices of these local people on the ground who are involved in this, and the affected community members themselves.' I don't think that's been taken very seriously. Yeah, I don't think that's been taken very seriously. In everything I've seen so far" (personal communication, independent observer, October 4, 2018).

During interviews, respondents not only commented generally on limited local input into ECW processes, but also told anecdotes that illustrated an absence of community participation. One story described a trip in which ECW director Yasmin Sharif traveled to a beneficiary-country to meet with stakeholders about educational support to refugees. Upon learning that only very high-level donors, government officials, and policymakers were in attendance, and no local NGOs or members of affected communities would be present, a representative from an international NGO paid out of pocket to ensure that country-level representatives could travel to the event and attend. In another anecdote, I was told about a recently proposed ECW program, in which the proposal had been designed completely free of any input from local actors. It planned a parallel non-formal education system, with "no discussion with the Ministry . . . no evidence, with no needs assessment . . . it was really appalling. It was sensationalist," and "unethical" (personal communication, independent observer, December 18, 2018).

The limited engagement with governments and local actors likely relates to ECW's goal of rapid response. The organization's mandate to deliver financing to education in emergency contexts naturally rests on an ability to approve and distribute funds in a quick and flexible way. As its strategic plan notes: "ECW's flexible investment modalities are geared to support a rapid response to urgent education needs" (ECW, 2018d, p. 5). And so this flexibility and speed is one way in which ECW adds value and offers a unique and much-needed platform. However, effective humanitarian aid practices that truly engage local actors require a great deal of due diligence. Respondents noted the appearance of a trade-off between rapidity and local consultation, observing that ECW country-level practices were

> driven by the urge of showing quickly that they could do the job and all of
> that. But the dialogue wasn't there . . . due to the urge of quick results and
> quick wins. . . . Also, the drive of getting a better engagement of non-donors,
> or recipient or Global South, it's still pretty remote I think, especially in the
> operations. I think they're not staffed strong enough to go out and do all the
> due diligence and they're too dependent on just jumping in and towing to
> the UN system and then expect that they can go ahead and create a program.
> (personal communication, bilateral donor, October 2, 2018)

Another interviewee explained: "I think it's meant with the best of intentions, but I think it's dangerous because it can enable for poor-quality intervention practices" (personal communication, independent observer, December 18, 2018).

Another structural impediment to local participation involves requirements for increasingly outcomes-based approaches and accountability mechanisms in order for donors to agree to fund them. Such external stringent pressures around outcomes have led to financing the established international agencies already operating in-country, as opposed to new, local actors. Moreover, logistics make local participation very challenging, including the time that must be allocated for traveling to meetings and the costs involved. But in spite of these challenges, practitioners widely understand that humanitarian interventions, including aid to education in emergencies, will not be effective without adequate local participation:

> [I]f you look at the minimum standards that guide the education in emergencies
> work, community participation is a foundational standard. That needs to be
> at the heart of anything that practitioners and policymakers do in the field of
> education in emergencies. (personal communication, independent observer,
> October 4, 2018)

Another respondent said:

> You have to have an organization who understands how to engage at the local
> level and how to make sure that everybody's getting heard and that you hear

the voices of, not only the government, but also civil society organizations and whatnot. . . . Otherwise it's not going to work. Otherwise, I think they tend to be donor-driven priorities, which might not be the same priorities at the local level. (personal communication, bilateral donor, October 2, 2018)

Beyond increasing the effectiveness of programs, local community participation also speaks to an ethical dimension of humanitarian practice, where stakeholders understand that those most affected by aid and donor policies ought to have a say in those programs that directly affect them, with respondents speaking of the need for empowerment and recipient rights.

North/South Power Hierarchies Within ECW

Rhetoric from ECW makes clear that the fund rests on equitable partnership-based practices within governance and country-level processes, including collaborative and coordinated activities, participatory decisionmaking, country ownership, and the engagement of affected communities. Guidance on humanitarian action echoes the importance of these foundations. For instance, a consultation report for the World Humanitarian Summit urged: "Humanitarians should draw on the knowledge of community leaders and local CSOs to better understand conflict and community dynamics" (WHS, 2014, p. 47), and the United Nations Office for the Coordination of Humanitarian Affairs (OCHA) stated that "in order for humanitarians to be accountable to the people they serve and ensure that aid is effective, community engagement should never be an option. Instead, it should be an integral part of every response from the onset of an emergency" (OCHA, 2017). Based on interviews with respondents, however, ECW practices do not adequately reflect these principles. Its initial design was driven by high-level actors from global organizations, with limited participation of practitioners and country-level stakeholders. Its governance body is arguably exclusive to primarily those organizations and actors with established and positive relationships to Gordon Brown, and the selection process has lacked transparency. UNICEF's hosting role has been questioned by several actors, particularly due to a potential conflict of interest, exacerbating competition in the sector. Overall, respondents view ECW as potentially working against a stated need for coordination. Finally, local government and community participation in ECW processes appears to remain limited.

Respondents generally agreed that the majority of ECW staff and stakeholders honestly desire increased coordination, collaboration, and community participation. Also frequently mentioned in interviews was the early stage of ECW, and that its staff and leadership are "still learning." At this point, power dynamics within the fund tend to reflect longstanding hierarchies where actors from the Global North and particular organizations tend to hold higher-level positions in decisionmaking bodies. Limited participation from local communities contrasts with the country-ownership goals of the fund, likely due to structural factors, such as logistical challenges, pressures of accountability in an outcomes-based environment, and the goal of a rapid response. This leaves actors from the Global North in positions of influence, with inadequate engagement by recipients of ECW funding.

THE EMPOWERING OF PRIVATE ACTORS IN EDUCATION CANNOT WAIT

The Aspirations of Private Engagement: Nontraditional Funding and Innovation

In light of its mandate to "transform the aid system," one of the earliest and most dominant goals of ECW has been to "generate and disburse new funding," which mainly denoted private-sector financing (ECW, 2018d, p. 5). The nonstate sector, particularly philanthropies and businesses, are viewed as *new donors* or *nontraditional* sources of funds. Resources for ECW were meant to come not only from traditional donors, but also from "the business and commercial sector; finance from foundations; [and] philanthropy of public-spirited individuals" (ODI, 2016, p. 22), in line with a "promise to harness [the] private sector's resources to achieve collective outcome in education in emergencies" (ECW, 2017b, p. 4). Its strategic plan outlines its unique ability to "[leverage] additional financing for education in emergencies," and states that "ECW works with emerging and non-traditional donors, private sector organizations and foundations, in addition to traditional donors" (p. 10). The fund's Strategic Objective 2 is "Increase financing for education in crisis," including from nontraditional sources.

As potential sources of new funds, ECW sees a range of possible ways for the private sector to engage, such as through "a pop-up facility that enables non-traditional funders such as the private sector and philanthropists to quickly and easily channel financial support to a specific country, region, or part of [a] country's national plan, without cumbersome procedures that often hinder timely support for education in emergencies" (ECW, 2016, p. 7). In a 2017 "Frequently Asked Questions" memo on "How can the private sector, foundation or philanthropies support ECW?" the first method listed is "Contribute Financial Resources: The private sector can provide philanthropic contributions [to] ECW so that it can respond immediately in an emergency. Companies could contribute to ECW or to specific emergencies. We encourage companies to creatively identify ways to engage in mobilizing resources, including through their corporate social responsibility or philanthropic initiatives, customer contributions, or employee and external matching campaigns" (ECW, 2017a, p. 3).

The private sector is widely envisaged as being central to the ECW's efforts. As Kevin Watkins, chief executive officer of Save the Children UK—a key ECW partner—states: "If successful, the ECW mechanism could do for the education of children facing emergencies what the global funds in health have done—namely, mobilise private sector engagement and facilitate high impact, value-for-money interventions through effective pooling of resources" (Watkins, 2016, pp. 21–22). In a *Huffington Post* op-ed, Gordon Brown made clear the importance of the private sector in supporting the fund: "[I]nside the humanitarian tent we need charities, philanthropists, businesses and social enterprises as well as governments and international agencies—not just one sector determining who gets to set the pace of progress. Not dogmatic dismissals writing off creative thinkers" (Brown, 2016b).

ECW presents a new and meaningful way for businesses to engage in global education, largely spurred by the Syrian refugee crisis. One respondent stated: "Many business leaders were saying, 'it's one of the worst humanitarian crises that we have ever faced, and no one has done anything. . . . It's time for business leaders to really step up and say we can change this. We must do something. We absolutely need this Fund' . . . a lot of them are relying on this idea that the private sector, the for-profit, private sector will actively contribute to this fund" (personal communication, business, June 21, 2016). Another explained that "one of the reasons to establish the fund is to provide a platform for private funding to be channeled, so that's an underlying key factor for establishing the fund" (personal communication, UN/multilateral agency, October 6, 2017).

Those from the nongovernmental sector, moreover, view the participation of business actors as an indirect way to elicit more political attention to the cause of refugee education. In referencing a high-level meeting at the World Humanitarian Summit, an NGO representative explained: "I think for the sector, it's quite important that at this political level, and that includes the private sector in a sense, that folks are standing up for education emergencies. I think it's connected to also why the political levels are taking notice as well. Those converge in a sense, and I think we needed that" (personal communication, NGO, July 17, 2016). The private sector has the capacity to garner attention from politicians who are central in decision-making on education in emergencies, in turn opening the door to the voices of NGOs.

The most prominent voice of business within ECW has been the Global Business Coalition for Education (GBC-E). Established in 2012, GBC-E is a partnership-based convening body that acts as an umbrella organization offering a voice for businesses involved in global education. Through co-ordination, communication, and showcasing successful business initiatives in education, GBC-E includes over 200 company members and promotes "companies to become part of a global movement of businesses committed to changing children's lives through education" (GBC-E, 2016b).

In recent years, GBC-E has articulated the need for a stronger focus on education in humanitarian contexts, most notably in response to the Syrian refugee crisis, by hosting a series of convening sessions on education in conflict settings and education for refugees. GBC-E has made explicit calls for the business community to lead in alleviating the impact of emergencies on education: "Business will play a major role in addressing these [humanitarian] issues as the international community looks to the private sector's ingenuity and experience in delivering solutions at scale" (GBC-E, 2016a).

Alongside governments and aid agencies, ECW is vocally supported by the GBC-E, which was a pivotal player in its initial establishment. In May 2015, GBC-E was commissioned to coordinate a consultation with business actors on funding education in contexts of crisis and emergency: "The consultation findings were clear: The business community supports the creation of a fund or financing mechanism to mobilize increased resources to address the crisis of education in emergencies" (GBC-E, 2015). As a respondent confirms: "the Global Business Coalition was highly involved in the development of that platform" (personal communication, NGO, July 17, 2016). GBC-E's role in ECW development has been "to explore the demand and need for the creation of the fund and make the business case for it" (personal communication, business, June 30, 2016). Since its establishment, ECW has had a clear and important relationship to the GBC-E.

GBC-E played a key role at the World Humanitarian Summit in Istanbul in May 2016, and prior to the summit, touted its member presence at the event: "GBC-Education members NRS International, Pearson, and Western Union will add to the Summit's private sector presence through special side events, exhibits, and virtual advocacy alongside the summit" (GBC-E, 2016a). GBC-E and others hosted a special breakfast meeting that brought together corporate leaders alongside high-level political actors to discuss global initiatives to support education in contexts of crisis (WHS, 2016). As one respondent described it: "It was very high level. You had the heads of all the UN agencies. Ban Ki-moon came to this breakfast and spoke. . . . I find it quite interesting to go to the GBC-E breakfast and the room is packed with people lined up trying to be there . . . listening and hearing these really senior-level [representatives] from the UN side and so forth, and then the CEOs of these major corporations talking about education in emergencies" (personal communication, NGO, July 17, 2016).

GBC-E maintains strong ties to ECW. As mentioned, its founder, Sarah Brown, is the wife of the UN Special Envoy on Education, and the organization has been represented at several high-level meetings on ECW and holds a seat on its HLSG. GBC-E also developed the Rapid Education Action (REACT) database, which acts as a hub for information on private resources of potential distribution to contexts of emergency "by bringing the know-how and resources from the business community to support partners" (GBC-E, 2018). The motivations for GBC-E members' engagement in

ECW are twofold "because they care and they realize not only that they're a social impact because they understood the implications of children being out of school, but for a business impact, it's a good business decision for them to invest" (personal communication, business, June 21, 2016).

Some respondents noted that private actors hold the potential for "introducing more innovative effective approaches" (e.g., personal communication, UN/multilateral agency, October 6, 2016). Others noted that stakeholders have been "saying, 'We really need your help. You have the talents. You have resources that we don't have'." (personal communication, bilateral donor, July 11, 2016), and that stakeholders wished to "see if we can identify partnerships between private-sector, NGOs and really highlight the variety of ways that [the] private sector could use their expertise and innovation ideas" (personal communication, business, June 30, 2016).

Conceiving of participation in ECW as a business investment, however, led some actors to think that, for example, "there's something a little shady about it" (personal communication, NGO, July 17, 2018). Moreover, questions remain concerning how business actors will feel about putting resources into ECW—a pool of funds that will be distributed perhaps without their direct consultation: "Those commitments of funding, is that writing a blank check, or is that a check with specific types of asks?" (personal communication, NGO, July 6, 2016). And others voiced caution about the degree to which the private sector might coordinate with other actors within ECW and agree to commit to tangible funding.

The Reality of Private Participation

Questions relating to corporate funding of ECW persist. The bulk of rhetoric concerning private-sector participation in ECW relates to financing, securing private resources, and viewing businesses and foundations as new, nontraditional sources of funding to ECW. However, at this time, only one foundation has committed funds to ECW, and not a single business has done so (ECW, 2018a). According to respondents, the more pressing concern for private actors is holding and retaining a place at the policymaking table in ECW governance. For instance, early on, the GBC-E circulated a memo to ECW stakeholders expressing that the coalition felt that it did not have an adequate voice in governing the fund. Respondents noted that businesses behave in a manner where they seek to have influence over ECW policy venues, but not via fiscal contributions. For instance: "I think they really wanted a seat at the table in decision-making and governance . . . a little bit of a, 'If you really want our funding, to be considered for ECW, we need to have a voice in decision-making'" (personal communication, NGO, October 4, 2018). Another noted that private funding "is still far away from being a possibility. There's no private company who really wants to provide cash funding for the Education Cannot Wait fund as such . . . I would say it's aspirational" (personal communication, bilateral donor, October 2, 2018). Another donor representative described feeling "cautiously optimistic" about private participation in ECW:

> It's my greatest hope that it is early, and that it is something that people are going to stick with, and they're going to figure out how to do better and move away from the fancy meetings in Europe and elsewhere and figure out more stuff to hang your hat on a little bit. [But] sometimes I feel like: Are we being really naïve? How much money could the private sector possibly even have for something like this, right? (personal communication, bilateral donor, July 11, 2016)

Responses from key informants directly contrast with the rhetoric of ECW, which touts the benefits of increased private engagement in the fund and education in the context of crisis more generally.

The Discourse of Private Actors in ECW

Based on the rhetoric of ECW and its leadership, nontraditional, private financing is a foundational component to the establishment and continued success of the fund, setting it apart from traditional financing mechanisms for education in emergencies, and in development more generally. Yet this aspiration of private funding has been met with a restrained response from the side of businesses, and to a slightly lesser degree, foundations. Yet private actors, most notably via GBC-E, have demanded a place at the policy table and to be granted opportunities to engage in ECW decisionmaking and governance processes. In this way, private-sector participation in ECW largely echoes GPE's situation.

Business actors are framed as contributing to ECW through their "ingenuity and experience" (GBC-E, 2016a), as "non-traditional" and "creative" funders who will "foster innovation and entrepreneurship in the identification of specific, relevant, and transformative solutions" (ECW, 2017a, p. 3) with the capacity to deliver "high impact" and "value-for-money interventions" (Watkins, 2016, pp. 21–22; Brown, 2016b). Sarah Brown presents partnerships with the private sector as necessary: "[W]e need to build these partnerships, make them stronger and find new ways to innovate as we aspire to achieve education for all" (TheirWorld, 2018). The discourse of the private sector prompts assumptions relating to business actors' identities as being more innovative, efficient, impactful, and creative than traditional aid actors. This discourse arguably has legitimized the engagement of private actors, granting them authority to participate in the education in emergencies space via ECW.

Private engagement in ECW reflects private authority, in which private-sector actors have been afforded a strong degree of legitimacy and are allowed into spaces of public policy decisionmaking, free from committing resources. I argue that ECW, as it relates to private participation and authority, reflects productive power, through the elevation of new voices into decisionmaking spaces based on, ostensibly, a prevalent discourse relating to the technical knowledge, creativity, and innovation that private actors bring. As discussed in Chapter 1, productive power operates through discourse and by legitimating particular forms of knowledge, shaping whose knowledge matters (Barnett & Duvall, 2005a). In the case of ECW, as with GPE, private actors have been framed in such a way that they have been granted legitimacy, a seat at the table, and the right to hold influence and power. The business actors in particular have been sought out to provide expertise, are envisaged as potential core financiers of education, and are increasingly invited into the policy space—or "harnessed" (ECW, 2017b, p. 4)—and so are empowered with authority and a legitimate voice.

CONCLUSION

This chapter's overview of ECW offers critiques of the fund, including several dimensions of power asymmetries and elevating the influence of the private sector, free from much return. Indeed, interviews that I conducted reflected a general uneasiness surrounding ECW from the perspective of those who have been engaged in both its establishment and current operations. At the same time, it is crucial that I make clear that at this time, ECW is a very young partnership, and those aspects that I criticize here feasibly result primarily from its very recent establishment. As was described to me, ECW is a moving target, and so its practices change rather quickly in response to critiques and assessments of what is working or not. Respondents repeatedly noted that the fund is indeed desperately needed, fills a clear gap, and its leaders have the best of intentions.

Most power imbalances likely derive from structural issues, such as logistical challenges and accountability constraints, along with the mandate for a speedy response making slower participatory processes impractical. Moreover, a degree of bias and established personal relationships led to the engagement of particular actors and organizations, resulting in the exclusion of others. And the role of the private sector presents a case of private authority, with business actors empowered and harnessed to participate in influential decisionmaking spaces, based largely on a particular discourse, which (as will be discussed further in the concluding chapter) reflects productive power.

As shown in Chapter 4, the GPE case exposes comparable power dynamics, albeit relating to different structural issues and historical foundations.

And the broader global education network similarly uncovers the power of particular players. In the final chapter of this book, I discuss the findings detailed through the three studies, with an aim to articulate how power dynamics unfold both within and across educational partnerships, as well as ways that the international community might start to reconceptualize partnerships for equity and true participation.

CHAPTER 6

Conclusion

Reconceptualizing Partnerships in International Aid to Education

To conclude this book, I offer a summary and bridge the evidence presented in the previous chapters, exploring the ways in which the findings tie together, speak to each other, and support an overarching argument relating to power dynamics in international aid to education. In this chapter, I map the conceptual framework first described in Chapter 1 onto findings drawn from the network analysis, Global Partnership for Education (GPE), and Education Cannot Wait Fund (ECW) cases, analyzing the book's conclusions through the lenses of structural power and productive power. I then provide a summative exploration of power dynamics in partnerships. Finally, I end this book with ways that researchers, policymakers, and practitioners might reconceptualize partnerships in international aid to education.

STRUCTURAL POWER IN PARTNERSHIPS: NORTH/SOUTH HIERARCHIES

Structural power clearly emerges in the research presented throughout this book. As described here, this power concerns positionality within a structure, and more specifically, actors' placement within a particular hierarchy. Based on the position occupied within this hierarchy, the various actors' interests, capacities, and resources are constituted through social interactions. This structure and its maintenance reinforce the power that some actors wield, as well as the disempowerment of those in lower hierarchical positions, shaping the influence that actors hold and their identities.

In Chapter 3, I illustrated the ways in which the aid environment has changed and offered a network conceptualization to capture its expansion, interconnectedness, and complexity. But, as several scholars argue, this network does not represent equality. In fact, a key contribution of network analysis is its ability to expose asymmetries and the various hierarchical positionalities of actors and entities. In particular, centrality can be considered an indicator of influence and reflects a particular position in a structure. In this way, the conception of centrality as power aligns with an understanding of structural power. The social network analysis (SNA) that I presented on international educational partnerships shows that those from the Global North (especially donors) hold the highest centrality measures and can be assessed as wielding power, in particular relative to recipients of funding in the Global South. The world maps created by the network analysis also make clear that most relationships flow North to South or North to North, with very little South to South. This network analysis also exposes the peripheral position of the private sector, which upon further examination based on qualitative evidence, in fact may denote a form of power as an *exit option*. The network structure shows actors' and organizations' positionalities, and from the positions they occupy, the degree of power they hold as well.

In Chapter 4, I explored GPE's history of reforms, governance dynamics, and country-level processes in order to determine the roles and relative influence of particular actors within this multistakeholder partnership (MSP). I find that the GPE retains a power dynamic akin to that of a traditional and widely critiqued aid architecture, in which actors situated in the Global North wield the most influence and have the most dominant voices in decisionmaking. I also discussed how historically constituted administrative roles, the wielding of funds, and the speaking of dominant languages, maintained through the GPE decisionmaking and aid distribution structure, reinforced this hierarchy.

As the case of the GPE has shown, in spite of attempts to reform the partnership into a more participatory sphere, power asymmetries remain, wherein those that in the past held positions of power have retained their dominant hierarchical standing. In spite of some notable efforts to elicit increased southern participation within the GPE governance and in its country-level processes, a North/South hierarchy endures, opposing the goals that the GPE was established to reach. Findings from the GPE case demonstrate structural power through exposing the deeply ingrained, hierarchical structure of the partnership.

In similar ways, the qualitative evidence from the study of ECW exposes another example of structural power. This case shows that ECW practices, where high-level actors and organizations situated in the Global North hold the most powerful positions while beneficiaries (including local governments and communities affected by emergencies) have participated in only a limited way, do not align with ECW policy rhetoric. Pressures relating to a time-sensitive, rapid-response mandate and an outcomes-based aid environment counter the ECW goals of country ownership. As with GPE, the ECW case reflects a hierarchy of influence in which particular actors from the Global North sit in positions of power, with inadequate engagement of recipients.

Each of these three sets of findings, therefore, exposes structural power both within educational partnerships and across them. The network analysis reveals that donors who wield funds hold central positions, and donors are also shown to be uppermost in the hierarchy of the GPE's governance and country-level processes. In contrast, the network analysis shows that recipient countries overall hold lower centrality measures, indicating that they have less influence within the educational partnership network. In the case of ECW, the roles of beneficiaries are also shown to hold limited influence, with only minimal engagement at country levels and in governance. Similarly, the developing-country partners (DCPs) of GPE have a limited voice in governance, and their ability to steer policy, even within countries, remains uncertain.

Both the GPE and ECW cases exemplify the power of northern-based multilateral agencies as hosts—the World Bank and UNICEF, respectively. The Bank's role largely results from its historical position as inextricably tied to GPE when it was a trust fund of the Bank. Despite rhetoric that portrays the GPE as an autonomous agency, the relationship between the partnership and the Bank remains exceptionally close, as the latter physically hosts the GPE Secretariat, with a staff officially designated as Bank employees. The World Bank is also the Grant Agent of the majority of GPE projects—a position that several interview respondents described as holding a large degree of influence over country-level projects.

Similarly, UNICEF, as host to the ECW, reflects a very close relationship, also as Secretariat staff employer and physical host to the offices, as well as being the ECW fund custodian. UNICEF has been deeply engaged with the ECW from its early design to the present day, despite criticisms that UNICEF's hosting role would create a conflict of interest, allowing the UN agency to wield a disproportionate degree of influence over ECW and benefit more than other agencies from ECW funding. Respondents voiced concerns that UNICEF's powerful position would elicit competition in the sector, rather than the coordinated response portrayed by ECW rhetoric. Based on the SNA described in Chapter 3, UNICEF and the World Bank are both among the top 20 most central entities in the partnership network (11th and 12th, respectively). Through the lens of these three separate data sets, two northern-based multilateral agencies hold particularly high positions in the partnership-based educational aid hierarchy.

The combined findings presented in Chapters 3, 4, and 5 identify which organizations tend to dominate and hold the most influential positions in educational partnerships. These overwhelmingly include those situated in the Global North—bilateral donors and multilateral agencies, in particular UNICEF and the World Bank. And conversely, those with the least influence and the lowest positions in the hierarchy are those situated in the Global South, especially recipients and beneficiaries of funding, including governments and local communities.

Beyond the identification of positionality within this hierarchy, the qualitative studies shed light on some reasons why particular organizations and actors attain, and often retain, positions of power. These include historically constituted roles, established relationships and favoritism, wealth and the wielding of funds, the ability to communicate in the dominant language, the ability to navigate logistical challenges and constraints, and the influence of an outcomes-based environment. Through various means and in a range of ways, driven by different factors and histories, power hierarchies remain entrenched within educational partnerships and shape the participation and capacity of actors, signifying structural power.

PRODUCTIVE POWER IN PARTNERSHIPS:
THE FRAMING OF THE PRIVATE SECTOR

In this research, I have presented the meaning of the category *private sector* and ideas that underpin it as reflecting productive power, where those actors representing foundations and companies have been readily framed in unproblematized ways to elicit beliefs around their legitimate roles in global educational partnerships. Again, productive power operates through the diffusion of discourses that thereby legitimate particular systems of knowledge, meanings of categories, and subjects. This discourse is normalized, and it shapes what actors recognize as reality, with signifying ideas that become taken for granted as fixed. Productive power operates through various norms, meanings, and social identities, which in turn affect actions (Barnett & Duvall, 2005c). Both within the GPE and ECW, a particular signification of the private sector has been perpetuated in organizational discourse, which reflects the wider discourse of the international aid environment, relating to certain characteristics, capacities, and knowledge.

In the case of GPE, private actors—including both foundations and companies—currently sit on its board of directors. The history leading to this inclusion of the private sector relates to an identification of particular shortcomings to the then-Fast Track Initiative (FTI) financing mechanisms. Private foundations were initially invited to participate because they were seen as having past experience, knowledge, and expertise around funding to fragile and conflict-affected states. Respondents noted a growing recognition of foundations' expertise and stated that philanthropists were seen as significant players.

As a Secretariat staff member described, educational aid mandates are seeing "a greater and greater emphasis" on private-sector participation (interview, Secretariat, August 14, 2014), reflecting an understanding that private actors are to be included in partnerships. This growing emphasis can be traced to experiences in the health sector. In GPE rhetoric, private actors were viewed as an "unrestricted source of funding" (GPE, 2010, p. 10).

Respondents frequently made reference to GPE partners and the Secretariat pushing for the private sector to act as "nontraditional donors" (interview, bilateral donor, January 20, 2014), even though little evidence showed that companies or foundations would play this role.

These drivers behind private engagement included a specific discourse and a categorization of private actors as holding a unique knowledge and expertise as nontraditional, significant stakeholders in global education. Such a discourse, pervading past and current GPE rhetoric, includes notions of efficiency, technical expertise, resources, advocacy power, new financing, and innovation. This discourse drives perceptions of private actors as legitimate partners who bring notable and important elements to the partnership. Yet, as evidenced by interview responses, private actors are not particularly engaged in GPE—they do not actively spearhead new initiatives, have not made notable impacts on GPE practices, and have not committed much in the way of funding. Private actors themselves state that their roles lack clarity. At the same time, this legitimating discourse has opened up space for the private sector to occupy positions on the GPE board of directors, its decisionmaking body, as well as communicating consistent messaging that frames private actors as overwhelmingly positive, as partners who ought to be embraced by other stakeholders. The private sector holds a degree of legitimacy within GPE based on a discursive framing that has shaped the roles and identities of private actors.

Private engagement in ECW reflects similar discourses. Private actors were involved in the onset of ECW, mainly via the Global Business Coalition for Education (GBC-E), which presented its members as holding "ingenuity and experience in delivering solutions at scale" (GBC-E, 2016a). A core impetus behind the establishment of ECW was to leverage a nontraditional source of funding, in contrast to the bureaucratic, inefficient traditional aid actors. ECW rhetoric frequently refers to private actors in a discourse denoting a unique and innovative partner, viewed as able to "creatively identify ways to engage" (ECW, 2017a, p. 3).

ECW rhetoric frames the private sector as holding unique abilities, with expectations of efficiency and effectiveness, that will lead to the design and implementation of "high impact" and "value-for-money interventions" (Watkins, 2016, pp. 21–22). Gordon Brown himself contrasts traditional educational aid actors to the private sector, whom he describes as "creative thinkers" (Brown, 2016a). Private actors fit into a different category from other aid partners, underpinned by notions eliciting sentiments of excitement, newness, and innovative advancements, separated from the sluggish, bureaucratic norm. By this framing, private actors are viewed as holding legitimate knowledge, and thereby the authority to engage in the education in emergencies space.

However, the private sector has yet to embody the nontraditional funding role thus far, and according to respondents, the likelihood of eliciting many resources from private actors remains slim. Private actors hold two seats on the ECW High-Level Steering Group (HLSG)—notably, the same number as beneficiary countries—and, according to interviews, the GBC-E remains a core player in ECW policy design. Together, the legitimating of private participation in governance based on discourse reflecting overwhelmingly positive potential inputs of private engagement present evidence of private authority within ECW.

The discourse of private-sector engagement in ECW is remarkably similar to that of GPE—evidence that this discourse is truly diffuse and extends throughout the sector. The fact that this discourse counters some ways that private actors appear to think of and frame themselves (namely, that they'll be core funders) reflects its strength, particularly its aspirational elements. Based on this framing, private actors are readily understood to be among the many players involved in educational aid that have the capacity to play particular roles, unquestioned technical expertise, and the ability to dispense unlimited funds. This discourse, however, does not match with reality. With productive power at work, "diffuse and contingent social processes produce particular kinds of subjects," and in these cases, private-sector actors have been fitted into fixed "meanings and categories" that have been "taken for granted" and made "ordinary" (Barnett & Duvall, 2005c, p. 57). Such assumptions, however, contrast with the reality presented both by data on private funding to partnerships and by qualitative evidence from interviews denying that private actors play such roles.

What is more, the assumptions embedded in this discourse arguably have become pervasive, accepted, and diffused throughout the educational partnership network. Although the quantitative network analysis presented in Chapter 3 cannot capture the nature of the discourse through which productive power works, it can bring to light the degree to which, and the routes through which, these systems of signification are diffused through "networks of social forces perpetually shaping one another" (Barnett & Duvall, 2005c, p. 55). Although private actors are not central in the network, how they are defined and characterized and how actors make meaning of their presence are distributed throughout a very wide and interconnected network. In this way, we can interpret the educational aid environment not only as a web of interconnected relationships, but also ideas, norms, and assumptions. In terms of this research, these ideas are exposed as relating to particular conceptions of the private sector, although other systems of meaning and signification are certainly also diffused throughout the network.

SHIFTING POWER DYNAMICS IN PARTNERSHIPS

A key similarity between structural and productive power relates to their constructivist underpinnings, where both forms of power result from working through social relations that constitute the relative positions of actors. Although structural power is observed in a more direct sense, in terms of relations within a hierarchy, and productive power works in diffuse ways, including through discourse, both "emphasize structure relative to purposeful agency" (Barnett & Duvall, 2005c, p. 49). This means that structural and productive power are not necessarily subject to change, even when actors alter their behavior and intentionally control their own actions toward each another. Both structural and productive power align with conceptions of constructivism, where the "underlying normative structures constitute actors' identities and interests," and when examined through the lens of Barnett and Duvall's conceptual framework, emphasize "how constitutive effects also are expressions of power" (2005c, p. 41).

Because of these constructivist foundations, structural and productive power dynamics are difficult to dismantle. Shifting structures and diffuse discourses arguably require broad transformation and buy-in from many actors and organizations, not small-scale individual actions. The critiques that I present on North/South dynamics, for instance, do not merely relate to the fact that northern actors are funders and southern actors recipients; rather, I say that these roles exist in a particular context—one that is driven by northern-dictated outcomes and northern-designed accountability systems. Furthermore, at every level (global, national, and local alike), northern actors engage in these processes and apply pressure, whether intentionally or unintentionally.

Respondents from a range of organizations and countries lamented this challenge, explaining that the power hierarchies pervading partnerships in global education are historically constituted, resulting from ingrained inequities, reinforced through decades of development policy and practice, and permeating all aspects of international development and aid—not only within the education sector, and not only within partnership-based organizations. This is perhaps why, despite notable and explicit efforts to engage southern, local voices, the North/South power hierarchy is preserved. If the overall structure of the aid architecture remains the same, these inequities are, according to some, inevitable:

> In some ways it's an inevitable dynamic of the foreign aid relationship. The
> donors are going to have the power, and developing country governments,
> and their civil society even less so, are going to be sort of subjugated in that
> relationship. . . . I don't think that it's realistic to expect multi-stakeholder
> partnerships to completely reverse that dynamic, to completely level out
> the playing field. I think that's not the right expectation. Maybe a better
> expectation is that it does a better job than pure bilateral foreign aid or
> foreign aid that is sort of a club of donors deciding their priorities and funding
> those priorities without input . . . there are inevitable power dynamics when

some wealthy and more powerful countries are giving money. (personal communication, CSO, June 7, 2017)

I think that the attempts [at Southern engagement] are genuine, and I think they [MSPs] really are trying to think about that. But I think they're flying in the face of, I don't know, 50, 60 years of development practice. . . . How rich and deep is the [Southern actors] contribution going to be? (personal communication, independent observer, January 31, 2014)

I think [the] way these things are designed some of the structural barriers make it impossible. I think to achieve that level of real Southern voice, your whole starting point will have to be different. . . . And I think that's part of the problem because, in most of these cases, they're not really true partnerships. (personal communication, UN/multilateral agency, September 20, 2018)

These responses reflect the belief that despite genuine efforts toward creating an equitable aid to education landscape, one that embraces southern voices and true partnership, the structure in which these partnerships operate sustains the traditional hierarchy.

Counteracting the diffusion of discourse related to the benefits of engaging the private sector also presents a daunting challenge. The rise of private authority is based on particular beliefs relating to the characteristics of private actors. But engaging private actors as true partners remains elusive in governance and financing, and at country levels. The mandates of business actors are different from most state-based organizations, and despite the rhetoric, private actors do not engage to the degree or in the ways that other stakeholders wish. The discourse that defines them has led private actors into these partnerships, but with minimal results, thereby presenting challenges and confusion for those who are expected to partner with them. As can be seen from the perspective of respondents:

The companies that we engage with are working on profit models, and so there has been some skepticism around partnership and engagement. They're representing themselves as [our agency's] partners when they're still for-profit structures or are looking for private margins for some of the materials they produce. It's made partnership a bit more fraught in terms of what it means to be a partner, what it means to work together and leveraging partnership to gain access or trust, or credibility. It's a big challenge for us. (personal communication, UN/multilateral agency, July 26, 2016)

I think everybody is very open and welcomes private-sector engagement and funding, but I think it's also . . . from where I sit, I have no sense so far how

much does it actually bring to the table? I think that's another piece that
is still not very clear. So far, what I've seen with the private sector is, the
term that comes to mind is 'little patches of green', and I'm not sure it's
adding up to a collective whole necessarily. . . . Then I see that kind of
[nontraditional funding] discussion as it migrates up in the political system
to higher-level people. (personal communication, bilateral donor, July 11,
2016)

I think a lot of companies, many companies want to contribute to education.
They actually see very clearly how and why education is connected to what
they do every day and how it's connected to the bottom line. They've really
struggled for decades in trying to figure out how to engage in education. They
couldn't find the right organizations. They couldn't find the right NGOs.
It was very confusing when they spoke with development agencies. . . .
Companies were very confused. Where is there point of entry into this? Where
can they actually contribute money and how can they know their dollars
are making an impact, because they ultimately need to report this back to
shareholders if it's a publicly traded company. (personal communication,
business, June 21, 2016)

Several respondents voiced the opinion that the private sector is a
player in global education who is here to stay. And based on the rise of
private engagement within educational partnerships, one might agree with
this sentiment. Yet as evidenced through the network analysis in the case of
GPE, private actors are not deeply engaged in all aspects of educational aid,
and based on qualitative evidence, they tend to participate mainly when
it benefits them. Nonetheless, they have been positioned in spaces where
they can use their private authority based on a legitimating discourse surrounding them. Productive power works through these discourses, and the
private authority, legitimacy, and influence that result appear to be very
challenging to change, pervading the education and development arenas
despite evidence that private actors do not truly reflect what the discourse
says about them.

Some respondents, in contrast, disagree that these power dynamics are
inevitable; they offer more optimistic outlooks on partnerships in international aid to education, indicating that partnerships are a move in the right
direction:

I think that the larger structures of international aid to education can or have
the potential to reinforce exploitative power dynamics, but I do not think
that this is inevitable. I think that partnerships can and must . . . contribute
to more equitable environments. (personal communication, independent
observer, December 18, 2018)

> It feels like [in MSPs] a decent amount of progress has been made in terms of at least opening up a space for conversation with the other stakeholders that didn't exist before, and that doesn't always exist with bilateral donor arrangements, that often doesn't exist, in my understanding and experience. (personal communication, NGO, June 7, 2017)

As I conclude this book, I take these more hopeful sentiments seriously. The findings and arguments that I have made thus far have been overwhelmingly critical of educational aid and can be interpreted as cynical, particularly the notion that change is very challenging and that inequities are potentially inevitable. As a respondent told me:

> What I always feel when I read . . . academic documents, when it becomes too much of a bashing of what goes wrong all over the world is, then I'm always thinking: it's correct, it's certainly good research and correct information. But then what does it help to have the bashing? There's a lot of bashing, but very little ideas on how to actually change it. Because the reality is not so easy to be changed. (personal communication, bilateral donor, October 25, 2018)

Despite the critiques offered throughout this book, I do not aim to merely "bash" the educational aid environment and the partnership-based organizations that operate within it. Instead, I hope to spur the existing partnerships to carve out the requisite time and make explicit efforts to self-reflect and evaluate themselves, addressing the power hierarchies that these case studies have brought to light. Next, I present some ways in which stakeholders that work within educational aid might reconceptualize partnerships and act to alter their structures and question the discourses that operate within them. Also, I offer hope for realistic change through which power hierarchies might begin to shift.

RECONCEPTUALIZING PARTNERSHIPS

At this time, few would dispute the assessment that most donors have failed to meet the goals set out in the Paris Declaration on Aid Effectiveness. As a 2012 progress report noted, the pillar of "ownership" had been met with only "partial progress" (OECD, 2012, p. 29), and donors have been less likely than recipient governments to adhere to the Paris principles (Abdel-Malek & Koenders, 2011). A 2013 evaluation on commitment to the Paris Declaration similarly stated that progress on ownership was "mixed" (UN, 2013, p. 27). Although the Busan Agreement, which sought to operationalize the Paris Declaration, stated that "[p]artnerships for development can only succeed if they are led by developing countries, implementing approaches that are tailored to country-specific situations and needs," very few countries report that recipient leadership actually takes place (OECD, 2012; Riddell, 2014).

The partnerships examined in this book underscore these claims, in that recipients of educational aid were rarely cited as leaders in either policy development or implementation processes, and donors and multilateral players overwhelmingly remained in the most central and powerful positions. When analyzed through constructivist conceptions of power, this imbalance stems not merely from financial arrangements, where donors in the Global North are on the giving end and southern recipients, naturally, are on the other end. This relationship is overlaid by a broader structure, reinscribed through widely accepted, outcomes-based accountability and compliance-driven mandates, in which donors deem it necessary to dictate policy and process within both governance and country-level forums. In both the GPE and ECW cases, donors—who "put in the money"—clearly demand particular outcomes and use their voices more readily, and with more sway, than others in decisionmaking spaces. Furthermore, private actors predominantly based in the Global North are deemed legitimate partners based largely on their fiscal clout and potential for giving resources, along with a discourse that labels them as creative, innovative, knowledgeable, and efficient.

The partnership aid structure, moreover, works to benefit the northern agencies who adopt the roles of hosts. In the cases of both GPE and ECW, the hosts of funds and Secretariats—namely, the World Bank and UNICEF—are perceived as holding a high degree of influence and retain particular advantages, sometimes eliciting critiques of conflicts of interest.

Southern participation does indeed occur, where recipient actors hold seats in governance, write national education-sector policy documents, and attend country-level forums. However, based on evidence gleaned from the case studies of GPE and ECW, this participation often can be described as surface, or symbolic, rather than genuine and full. This symbolic participation emerges through respondents' reflections on the board-level dynamics of GPE, the design of in-country Education-Sector Plans (ESPs), the roles of beneficiaries in ECW design and governance, and the engagement of those affected by crises. In each case, the participation of southern, recipient actors is reported to be minimal, nonexistent, merely symbolic, or subjugated by voices of those from the Global North.

However, I maintain a view that this hierarchy need not be inevitable, and partnerships indeed have the potential to ameliorate North/South inequities. And so a question must be posed: How might partnerships be reconceptualized to ensure genuine, true partnership? Next, I present a few possible responses, including questions that actors and organizations might ask themselves when initiating partnerships and developing their policies, agreements, and strategic plans.

Apply a Network Approach

In Chapter 3, I argued for a reconceptualization of the aid architecture, which is now characterized by growing numbers of increasingly diverse actors with relationships to one another, as well as new and more complex mechanisms of aid distribution. Analyses of aid to education, especially in the context of partnerships, must not be made through the lens of the traditional donor–recipient relationship if researchers wish to truly grapple with the complexity of the current era and accurately assess power dynamics. I showed that a network approach allows an empirical, quantitative analysis of power across partnerships. This network analysis served to describe the network structure and show the relative centrality of various actors, from which an examination of power can be made.

This network approach, applied in this book from a scholarly perspective, also can be adopted in development practice to show stakeholders the reality of relationships and power dynamics in their own organizations and partnerships. SNA can be applied to address these dynamics through rethinking networked arrangements. Relationships and roles can then be readjusted to become more equitable. Given that networks expose what is happening, who is central, and who is truly on the periphery, network analyses of on-the-ground programs can reveal power dynamics, motivating actors to make discernable changes to the network structure. This rethinking of networked arrangements can lead to structures becoming more equitable.

Some examples of network analysis that have already been applied to development and humanitarian practice include the strengthening of communities for disaster resilience (Magsino, 2009); understanding the post-earthquake physical rehabilitation response in Haiti (Tataryn & Blanchet, 2012); the impacts of social relationships on microeconomic development programs in Timor-Leste (Dale, 2011); and the sustainability of alliances in the rural South Caucasus (Oxfam, 2016).[1] As described in Chapter 3, several scholars have studied power relationships in international relations and development using SNA, but less so by practitioners. When applied in practice, moreover, practitioners can compare the rhetoric of their organizations and the ways in which partnership structures are mapped out formally to the way they look in reality. Such comparisons can inform revisions of partnership-based policies to ensure that those in the most central positions represent local actors and communities, rather than donors and those predominantly from the Global North.

A network approach can also be applied by global partnerships to inform self-studies, and in turn determine the centrality of stakeholders and the ties between them. These studies can be based on both quantitative and qualitative data, where interviews about relationships (both formal and informal) and influence can inform the analysis (see Faul, 2016b). If partnerships viewed themselves as networks in practice, the application of SNA can be enormously beneficial for visualizing, understanding, and changing power dynamics. Self-evaluations that employ a network approach can allow organizations to ask such questions as: To what degree does this network exhibit an equitable space? Put another way, are particular actors disproportionately central in the network? Who is located more peripherally, and what might these positions in the network indicate?

Elicit Active and Equitable Participation

The cases of both GPE and ECW expose the participation of southern beneficiaries of funding as often being minimal or merely symbolic. According to the INEE's Minimum Standards for Education (INEE, 2010):

> There are various degrees and forms of participation. Symbolic participation ranges from use of services to acceptance of decisions made by others. Full participation refers to the active contribution of time and direct involvement in decisionmaking, planning and implementation of education activities. Experience has shown that symbolic participation alone is not effective in providing quality and lasting education responses. . . . International humanitarian stakeholders should offer support and capacity building to education authorities, civil society organisations and local actors, taking care not to infringe on their legitimate roles. (p. 20)

Symbolic participation occurs when actors are included physically in a space, but without mechanisms in place to ensure that their legitimate voices are heard. A frequent theme arising in interviews with stakeholders involved in both GPE and ECW was the symbolic representation of southern-based beneficiaries, who are touted by the organizations as partners based on their seats in governance, but wielding far less influence, positioned as the least dominant voices in decisionmaking, and facing consistent logistical constraints that work against their active participation.

Full participation of southern, recipient partners must occur at all stages—in the design of a partnership, in its governance body, in its administrative hosting relationship, and at the country level in aid distribution, implementation, and policy design. All stakeholders must be conscious of the need for active participation and apply strategies to address power asymmetries. Perhaps, through applying network analysis strategies, one can understand and be conscious of who is in power and who has legitimate voice and influence.

One mechanism for ensuring active participation is the inclusion of southern-based civil society actors, who represent recipient countries but are free from some of the challenges faced by recipient governments. As a respondent explains, "Civil society does have a unique voice. We essentially are allowed to speak more freely. We are not as hand-tied by the government that we represent, or any kind of broader, institutional positions that representatives may feel bound by" (personal communication, CSO, September 12, 2018).

Active participation is, needless to say, far more challenging to ensure than symbolic participation. One respondent relayed an experience developing guidance on education, and explained that for the process to be inclusive, it took much more time, but the outcome was successful as a result:

> [I]t was going to be a shorter process, but it ended up taking us two years because there was really a commitment to local voices. It meant that, to do a series of four regional consultations, anyone at those regional consultations had to hold local consultations or national consultations with local actors. It meant we had to do a lot of fundraising for different groups, and so all those processes took so much longer, but I feel like it's why the [outputs] are still relevant today and that people still use them and talk about them, you know, 10 years later, 15 years later, because that kind of involvement meant that whatever it was, whatever came out of that, was owned by local communities. And it was hard to do. (personal communication, independent observer, October 4, 2018)

A key critique of ECW was the apparent conflict between speed and participation, where rapid response is viewed as prioritized over and above local consultation. As the quotation given here indicates, active participation takes time and may be a less predictable and lengthy process, but it is worthwhile for its impact and for true engagement of those affected. OCHA (2017) observes, "In any emergency, time is always of the essence. Lifesaving assistance needs to be provided quickly, and taking the time to consult with people may seem counterproductive," but community engagement helps to enable access to affected peoples, supports efficient distribution of aid, and ensures long-term recovery and resilience. As Riddell (2014) further explains: "A key ingredient to providing effective aid is in-depth local knowledge, an issue of fundamental importance if aid is to make an effective contribution to building local expertise and ownership" (p. 40).

Active participation at country levels, moreover, requires trust in local partners. For example, a respondent shared an anecdote in which a local partner implementing a program asked for a large amount of coffee to be budgeted into program costs. When the international funder pressed for a justification, the local actor replied, "'[B]ecause we found the most effective way to talk to mothers was to give them a cup of coffee'. . . . So whatever. It's not my business. And I think that's fundamentally the difference. As a program manager sitting here, I have to trust my partner. I have to trust my partner to know that if he needs 15 kilos of coffee, fine" (personal communication, independent observer, December 18, 2018).

Yet this trust appears to be rare. It requires that northern actors relinquish some control over development processes, which is made even more challenging in the outcomes-based accountability environment under which most of them operate. For example, a study on country ownership in Africa reported: "Donor officials in recipient countries often doubt the competence and probity of African civil servants and politicians, and are therefore reluctant to let go of their control. Donor country staff are also constrained by the incentive structure within donor agencies compelling them to 'deliver' on targets which are often beyond their influence" (de Renzio, Whitfield, & Bergamaschi, 2008, p. 4).

Symbolic participation takes less time and allows northern actors to continue operating to serve outcomes-based mandates within an existing, predicable structure. But only active, full participation ensures true country ownership and can engender genuine, equitable partnerships. Upon embarking on new initiatives that seek to engage southern and local community actors, partnerships might reflect upon and ask whether they are eliciting full, active participation. Are local actors embraced as leaders? Are southern actors driving policy development and decisionmaking? And, by contrast, are northern actors disproportionately benefiting from participating in the partnership relative to other parties?

Question the Discourse

This book has shed light on the growing role of the private sector in global partnerships and some widespread beliefs regarding the capacities, resources, and knowledge that business actors can bring. These beliefs rest on a particular aspirational discourse frequently applied to the private sector relating to technical know-how, efficiency, creative thinking, innovation, and wielding large sums of money that can be readily disbursed to support education. Yet the GPE and ECW cases suggest that this discourse ought to be questioned, particularly given the limited engagement of the private sector in supporting new initiatives and the even more pronounced nominal commitment to funding.

The case studies make clear that the discourse categorizing the private sector in a particular way lacks grounding in evidence and does not match the motivations of private actors themselves for engagement. Private actors have voiced reluctance to fiscally support global partnerships and also to engage deeply in activities. They do, however, wish to hold a seat at the table and ostensibly to have a voice in major decisionmaking in partnership governance. Private actors (in particular, companies), however, appear to be largely concerned with advancing profit-oriented agendas and join in partnerships to solidify relationships with actors who have the capacity to implement their initiatives. By evaluating private-sector motives, and through investigating the likelihood that private actors will fulfill certain roles, partnership stakeholders can better assess whether to embrace business actors as partners. This would require a questioning of the discourse that has labeled private actors in a broadly positive way, as well as unpacking the assumptions that drive this discourse.

Questioning this discourse can be supported by a wide array of scholarship that has included critical analyses of private-sector participation in the international education policy arena,[2] which offer findings from a range of empirical studies that together call into question the taken-for-granted framing of the value of private-sector engagement. In addition, several organizations (most notably NGOs) have supported research that has served to spur critical questions of the roles that private actors play in global education.[3] Although the purpose of this book was not to offer critiques of private-sector activities per se, my findings do act as a springboard for questioning private participation in partnerships through exposing the ways in which business actors have been empowered and gained legitimacy and authority. In questioning the ways in which particular actors are presented and envisioned in policy discourse and institutional rhetoric, organizations might ask: Is this discourse based on evidence, or assumptions and aspirations? And who might be disproportionately empowered by this discourse?

CONCLUSION

I have written this book for two primary audiences: first, scholars (including researchers, academics, instructors, and students) of comparative and international education, global governance, and international development and relations; and second, practitioners in the fields of education, development, and humanitarianism, working at both the global policy and country levels. I sincerely hope that with this book, I have introduced for both audiences some new ways of thinking about and analyzing the current era in international aid to education, while also prompting some shifts in beliefs around their taken-for-granted assumptions. Although I present this work from a highly critical perspective, I wish to close by reiterating that I believe partnerships hold value, and at their foundation, they offer promising moves in the right direction for international aid actors and organizations.

Much of the analysis in this book is based on interviews with key informants. I say without hesitation that I believe each of the more than 50 people who graciously accepted my invitation to participate in this research genuinely wants to improve aid to education and believes that recipients of aid deserve more dominant voices and the right to full participation in equitable spaces. To achieve these goals, however, stakeholders must overcome longstanding structures and prevalent discourses. Despite these challenges, the aid environment clearly evolves, and the actors within it are eager for positive change.

NOTES

1. See Chapter 16 of Ramalingam (2013) for a comprehensive review of network analysis as applied in development practice.

2. See, for example, Adamson, Astrand, and Darling-Hammond (2016), Ball (2012), Bulkley and Burch (2011), Verger, Fontdevila, and Zancajo (2016), and Steiner-Khamsi and Draxler (2018).

3. These organizations include ActionAid, Education International, Open Society Foundation, and Oxfam International.

References

Abdel-Malek, T., & Koenders, B. (2011). *Progress towards more effective aid: What does the evidence show?* Retrieved from www.oecd.org/dac/effectiveness /48966414.pdf

Abrahamsen, R. (2004). The power of partnerships in global governance. *Third World Quarterly, 25*(8), 1453–1467. Retrieved from doi.org/10.1080/014365 9042000308465

Adams, B., & Judd, K. (2018). *The 2030 agenda, donor priorities and UN mandates: Lessons from the WHO experience.* Bonn, Germany: Global Policy Forum. Retrieved from www.globalpolicywatch.org

Adams, B., & Martens, J. (2016). *Partnerships and the 2030 agenda: Time to reconsider their role in implementation.* Retrieved from www.globalpolicywatch.org /blog/2016/05/23/partnerships-and-the-2030-agenda-time-to-reconsider-their -role-in-implementation

Adamson, F., Astrand, B., & Darling-Hammond, L. (Eds). (2016). *Global education reform: How privatization and public investment influence education outcomes.* New York, NY: Routledge.

Arnstein, S. (1969). A ladder of citizen participation. *AIP Journal, 35*(4), 216–224.

Bäckstrand, K. (2006). Multi-stakeholder partnerships for sustainable development: Rethinking legitimacy, accountability and effectiveness. *European Environment, 16*(5), 290–306. Retrieved from doi.org/10.1002/eet.425

Bäckstrand, K. (2008). Accountability of networked climate governance: The rise of transnational climate partnerships. *Global Environmental Politics, 8*(3), 74–102.

Ball, S. J. (2009). Privatising education, privatising education policy, privatising educational research: Network governance and the "competition state." *Journal of Education Policy, 24*(1), 83–99. Retrieved from doi.org/10.1080 /02680930802419474

Ball, S. J. (2010). New states, new governance and new education policy. In M. W. Apple, S. J. Ball, & L. A. Gandin (Eds.), *The Routledge international handbook of the sociology of education* (pp. 155–166). London, UK: Routledge.

Ball, S. J. (2012). *Global education Inc: New policy networks and the neo-liberal imaginary.* New York, NY: Routledge.

Ball, S. J., & Junemann, C. (2012). *Networks, new governance and education.* Bristol, UK: Policy Press.

Barnes, A., & Brown, G. W. (2011). The idea of partnership within the Millennium Development Goals: Context, instrumentality and the normative demands of

partnership. *Third World Quarterly*, 32(1), 165–180. Retrieved from doi.org
/10.1080/01436597.2011.543821

Barnes, A., Brown, G. W., & Harman, S. (2016). Understanding global health and
development partnerships: Perspectives from African and global health system
professionals. *Social Science & Medicine*, 159, 22–29. Retrieved from doi.org
/10.1016/j.socscimed.2016.04.033

Barnett, M., & Duvall, R. (2005a). Power in global governance. In M. Barnett &
R. Duvall (Eds.), *Power in global governance*, (pp. 1–32). Cambridge, UK:
Cambridge University Press.

Barnett, M., & Duvall, R. (2005b). *Power in global governance*. Cambridge, UK:
Cambridge University Press.

Barnett, M., & Duvall, R. (2005c). Power in international politics. *International
Organisation*, 59(1), 39–75.

Barnett, M., & Finnemore, M. (2005). The power of liberal international organizations. In M. Barnett & R. Duvall (Eds.), *Power in global governance*,
(pp. 161–184). Cambridge, UK: Cambridge University Press.

Beckfield, J. (2008). The dual world polity: Fragmentation and integration in the
network of intergovernmental organisations. *Social Problems*, 55(3), 419–442.

Bennett, A. (2010). Process tracing and causal inference. In H. Brady & D. Collier
(Eds.), *Rethinking social inquiry* (pp. 207–220). Lanham, MD: Rowman and
Littlefield.

Bezanson, K. A., & Isenman, P. (2012). *Governance of new global partnerships: Challenges weaknesses and lessons*. Washington, DC: Center for Global Development.

Bezanson, K. A., Narain, S., & Prante, G. (2004). *Independent evaluation of CGIAR
partnership*. Retrieved from library.cgiar.org/handle/10947/631

Bhanji, Z. (2008). Transnational corporations in education: Filling the governance
gap through new social norms and market multilateralism? *Globalisation,
Societies and Education*, 6(1), 55–73.

Bhanji, Z. (2012). Transnational private authority in education policy in Jordan
and South Africa: The case of Microsoft Corporation. *Comparative Education
Review*, 56(2), 300–319.

Borgatti, S. P., Everett, M., & Johnson, J. (2013). *Analyzing social networks*. Los
Angeles: Sage.

Borgatti, S. P., & Halgin, D. S. (2011). Analyzing affiliation networks. In J. Scott
& P. J. Carrington (Eds.), *Sage handbook of social network analysis* (pp. 417–
433). London, UK: Sage.

Borgatti, S. P., Mehra, A., Brass, D. J., & Labianca, G. (2009). Network analysis
in the social sciences. *Science*, 323(5916), 892–895. Retrieved from doi.org/10
.1126/science.1165821

Boston Consulting Group (BCG). (2016). *ECW operational manual & results
framework: Consultation process and overview*. Retrieved from www.educat
ioncannotwait.org/wp-content/uploads/2016/05/ECW-Overview-for-Country
-Consultations.pdf

Boston Consulting Group (BCG). (2017). *Press release: BCG wins award for work
with first global fund for education in emergencies*. Retrieved from www.bcg
.com/d/press/15september2017-bcg-award-consulting-mag-education-171065

Brock-Utne, B. (2001). Education for all—in whose language? *Oxford Review of
Education*, 27(1), 115–134.

Brookings. (2018). *Are impact bonds and outcome funds a solution to the global learning crisis?* Retrieved from www.brookings.edu/blog/education-plus-develop ment/2018/06/18/are-impact-bonds-and-outcome-funds-a-solution-to-the-global -learning-crisis

Brown, G. W. (2010). Safeguarding deliberative global governance: The case of the Global Fund to Fight AIDS, Tuberculosis and Malaria. *Review of International Studies, 36,* 511–530.

Brown, G. (2016a). *Project syndicate: New ways to finance education.* Retrieved from www.project-syndicate.org/commentary/new-ways-finance-education-by -gordon-brown-2015-06

Brown, G. (2016b). *To really help Syria, we should start with a bold new humanitarian vision like this.* Retrieved from www.huffingtonpost.com/gordon-brown /humanitarian-aid-syria_b_9195800.html

Bulkley, K., & Burch, P. (2011). The changing nature of private engagement in public education: For-profit and nonprofit organizations and educational reform. *Peabody Journal of Education, 21*(1), 155–184.

Buse, K., & Tanaka, S. (2011). Global public-private health partnerships: Lessons learned from ten years of experience and evaluation. *International Dental Journal, 61*(2), 2–10.

Cambridge Education, Mokoro, & Oxford Policy Management. (2010). *Mid-term evaluation of the EFA Fast Track Initiative: A final synthesis.* Retrieved from https:// www.globalpartnership.org/content/mid-term-evaluation-efa-fast-track-initiative

Chabbott, C. (2003). *Constructing education for development: International organizations and education for all.* London, UK: Routledge Falmer.

Cities Alliance. (2018). *Governance.* Retrieved from: https://www.citiesalliance.org /index.php/who-we-are/about-cities-alliance/governance-0

Clarke, M. (2018, August 2). *Global South: What does it mean and why use the term?* Retrieved from onlineacademiccommunity.uvic.ca/globalsouthpolitics/2018/08 /08/global-south-what-does-it-mean-and-why-use-the-term

Colclough, C. (2000). Who should learn to pay? An assessment of neo-liberal approaches to education policy. In C. Colclough & J. Manor (Eds.), *States or markets? Neo-liberalism and the development policy debate* (pp. 197–213). Oxford, UK: Clarendon Press.

Collier, D. (2011). Understanding process tracing. *Political Science and Politics, 44*(4), 823–830.

Cooper, A. (2014). Knowledge mobilisation in education across Canada: A cross-case analysis of 44 research brokering organisations. *Evidence & Policy: A Journal of Research, Debate and Practice, 10*(1), 29–59. Retrieved from doi .org/10.1332/174426413X662806

Cornwall, A. (2008). Unpacking "participation": Models, meanings and practices. *Community Development Journal, 43*(3), 269–283.

Cox, R. (1992). Multilateralism and world order. *Review of International Studies, 18,* 161–180.

Crawford, G. (2003). Partnership or power? Deconstructing the "Partnership for Governance Reform" in Indonesia. *Third World Quarterly, 24*(1), 139–159. Retrieved from doi.org/10.1080/713701365

Dados, N., & Connell, R. (2012). The Global South. *Contexts, 11*(1), 12–13. doi .org/10.1177/1536504212436479

Dale, P. (2011, June 28). *Ties that bind: Studying social networks in Timor-Leste.* Retrieved from blogs.worldbank.org/publicsphere/ties-bind-studying-social-net works-timor-leste

de Renzio, P., Whitfield, L., & Bergamaschi, I. (2008, June). *Reforming foreign aid: What country ownership is and what donors can do to support it.* Global economic governance briefing paper. Retrieved from www.geg.ox.ac.uk/publication /reforming-foreign-aid-practices-what-country-ownership-and-what-donors -can-do-support

Deutscher, E., & Jacquet, P. (2010, October 17). *Addressing the overcomplexity of international aid architecture.* Retrieved from publish.indymedia.org/fr/2010 /10/942389.shtml

Dryden-Peterson, S. (2016). Policies for education in conflict and post-conflict reconstruction. In K. Mundy, A. Green, R. Lingard, & A. Verger (Eds.), *Handbook of global policy and policy-making in education* (pp. 189–205). West Sussex, UK: Wiley-Blackwell.

Education Cannot Wait (ECW). (2016). *Case for investment.* Retrieved from s3 .amazonaws.com/inee-assets/resources/ECW_-_Investment_Case_EN.pdf

Education Cannot Wait (ECW). (2017a). *Frequently asked questions.* Retrieved from www.educationcannotwait.org/wp-content/uploads/2017/02/ECW-Draft -FAQs-_Feb-2017-1.pdf

Education Cannot Wait (ECW). (2017b). *Update on 2017 progress.* Retrieved from www.agendaforhumanity.org/sites/default/files/resources/2018/Jun/Initiati ves%20Updates_ECW_final_22%20June.pdf

Education Cannot Wait (ECW). (2018a). *About ECW.* Retrieved from www.edu cationcannotwait.org/about-ecw

Education Cannot Wait (ECW). (2018b). *Grantee operating manual.* Retrieved from s3.amazonaws.com/inee-assets/resources/Grantee-Operating-Manual.pdf

Education Cannot Wait (ECW). (2018c). *High-Level Steering Group terms of reference.* Retrieved from www.educationcannotwait.org/wp-content/uploads/2016 /05/High-Level-Steering-Group-Terms-of-Reference.pdf

Education Cannot Wait (ECW). (2018d). *Strategic plan.* Retrieved from www .educationcannotwait.org/wp-content/uploads/2018/05/Strategic_plan_2018 _2021_web_PAGES.pdf

Edwards, D. B., & Klees, S. (2015). Unpacking "participation" in development and education governance: A framework of perspectives and practices. *Prospects, 45*(4), 483–499.

Edwards, S. (2018a). *International finance facility for education musters growing support.* Retrieved from www.devex.com/news/international-finance-facility -for-education-musters-growing-support-93523

Edwards, S. (2018b). *Is the global education sector heading toward fragmentation?* Retrieved from www.devex.com/news/is-the-global-education-sector-heading -toward-fragmentation-93270

Edwards, S. (2018c). *Plans for the international finance facility for education take shape.* Retrieved from www.devex.com/news/plans-for-the-international-finance -facility-for-education-take-shape-92725

Education Commission. (2019). *Explore the learning generation report.* Retrieved from educationcommission.org/international-finance-facility-education

Education Outcomes Fund (EOF). (2019). *Home page*. Retrieved from www.edu cationoutcomesfund.org

Estabrooks, C. A., Dersken, L., Winther, C., Lavis, J. N., Scott, S. D., Wallin, L., & Profetto-McGrath, J. (2008). The Intellectual Structure and Substance of the Knowledge Utilization Field: A longitudinal author co-citation analysis, 1945–2004. *Implementation Science, 3*(49).

Evans, A. (2012). *Report of the hosting review*. Washington, DC: Global Partnership for Education (GPE).

Faul, M. V. (2016a). *Multi-sectoral partnerships and power*. Geneva, Switzerland: United Nations Research Institute for Social Development.

Faul, M. V. (2016b). Networks and power: Why networks are hierarchical not flat and what can be done about it. *Global Policy, 7*(2), 185–197.

Faul, M. V., & Tchilingirian, J. (2018, April). *Power and multistakeholderism: The structuring of spaces between fields*. Paper presented at the International Studies Conference 2018, San Francisco.

Fengler, W., & Kharas, H. (2011) Delivering aid differently: Lessons from the field. *Economic Premise*. 49. Retrieved from www.worldbank.org/economicpremise

Finnemore, M. (2014). Dynamics of global governance: Building on what we know. *International Studies Quarterly, 58*(1), 221–224.

Finnemore, M., & Sikkink, K. (2001). Taking stock: The constructivist research program in international relations and comparative politics. *Annual Review of Political Science, 4*, 391–416.

Foucault, M. (1982). The subject and power. *Critical Inquiry, 8*(4), 777–795.

Fowler, A. (2000). Introduction beyond partnership: Getting real about NGO relationships in the aid system. *IDS Bulletin, 31*(3), 1–13. Retrieved from doi.org /10.1111/j.1759-5436.2000.mp31003001.x

Frenk, J., & Suerie, M. (2013). Governance challenges in global health. *The New England Journal of Medicine, 368*(10), 936–942.

GAIN. (2018). *Organization Governance*. Retrieved from: https://www.gainhealth .org/organization/governance/

GAVI. (2018). *Board composition*. Retrieved from: https://www.gavi.org/about /governance/gavi-board/members/

Gill, S., & Law, D. (1989). Global hegemony and the structural power of capital. *International Studies Quarterly, 33*(4), 475–499.

GIZ. (2018). *About GIZ*. Retrieved from www.giz.de/en/html/about_giz.html

Global Business Coalition for Education (GBC-E). (2015). *Policy brief: A fund for education in emergencies: Business weighs in*. Retrieved from gbc-education .org/wp-content/uploads/2015/06/Policy-Brief-Education-in-Emergencies .pdf

Global Business Coalition for Education (GBC-E). (2016a). *First-ever World Humanitarian Summit to scale up the business response in crisis*. Retrieved from gbc-education.org/world-humanitarian-summit

Global Business Coalition for Education (GBC-E). (2016b). *Mission*. Retrieved from gbc-education.org/mission

Global Business Coalition for Education (GBC-E). (2018). *Rapid Education Action Initiative (REACT): Education in emergencies*. Retrieved from gbc-education .org/wp-content/uploads/2018/09/GBC-Education-REACT.pdf

Global Campaign for Education (GCE). (2008). *At the crossroads: Which way forward for a global compact on education?* Retrieved from www.campaign foreducation.org/docs/reports/At%20the%20crossroads%20Which%20 way%20forward%20for%20a%20global%20compact%20on%20educa-tion.pdf

Global Campaign for Education (GCE). (2014). *About us.* Retrieved from www .campaignforeducation.org/en/about-us

Global Campaign for Education (GCE), & Oxfam. (2012). *A more ambitious, effective Global Partnership for Education: Three priorities for the next phase of reform.* Retrieved from www.campaignforeducation.org/en/resources

Global Fund. (2011). *Turning the page from emergency to sustainability: The final report of the high-level independent review panel on fiduciary controls and oversight mechanisms of the global fund to fight AIDS, tuberculosis and malaria.* Retrieved from https://www.theglobalfund.org/media/5424/bm25_high levelpanelindependentreviewpanel_report_en.pdf?u=636917017430000000

Global Partnership for Education (GPE). (2010). *Suggestions for FTI board composition.* Retrieved from www.globalpartnership.org/content/suggestions-fti -board-composition-29-april-2010

Global Partnership for Education (GPE). (2011, November). *Statement from private sector and private foundations.* Statement presented at Global Partnership for Education board of director's meeting, Copenhagen.

Global Partnership for Education (GPE). (2012). *Constituency composition on the board of directors—Paris.* Retrieved www.globalpartnership.org/content/consti tuency-composition-board-directors

Global Partnership for Education (GPE). (2013a). *Charter of the Global Partnership for Education.* Washington, DC: Author.

Global Partnership for Education (GPE). (2013b). *Report of the Chief Executive Officer—Addis Ababa.* Retrieved from www.globalpartnership.org/content/chief -executive%E2%80%99s-report-meeting-board-directors-addis-ababa-ethiopia

Global Partnership for Education (GPE). (2015). *A platform for education in crisis and conflict: A GPE issues paper.* Retrieved from www.globalpartnership.org /content/platform-education-crisis-and-conflict-gpe-issues-paper

Global Partnership for Education (GPE). (2016a). *Aid effectiveness.* Retrieved from www.globalpartnership.org/focus-areas/aid-effectiveness

Global Partnership for Education (GPE). (2016b). *Developing countries.* Retrieved from www.globalpartnership.org/about-us/developing-countries

Global Partnership for Education (GPE). (2016c). *GPE 2020 Strategic Plan.* Retrieved from www.globalpartnership.org/content/gpe-2020-strategic-plan

Global Partnership for Education (GPE). (2016d). *Pledges.* Retrieved from www .globalpartnership.org/funding/replenishment/pledges

Global Partnership for Education (GPE). (2018a). *Charter of the Global Partnership for Education.* Retrieved from www.globalpartnership.org/content/charter -global-partnership-education

Global Partnership for Education (GPE). (2018b). *Developing country partners.* Retrieved from www.globalpartnership.org/about-us/developing-countries

Global Partnership for Education (GPE). (2018c). *Private sector.* Retrieved from www.globalpartnership.org/about-us/private-sector

Goddard, S. E. (2009). Brokering change: Networks and entrepreneurs in international politics. *International Theory*, *1*(2), 249. Retrieved from doi.org/10.1017/S1752971909000128

Goldie, D., Linick, M., Jabbar, H., & Lubienski, C. (2014). Using bibliometric and social media analyses to explore the "Echo Chamber" hypothesis. *Educational Policy*, *28*(2), 281–305. Retrieved from doi.org/10.1177/0895904813515330

Guijt, I. (2010). Rethinking monitoring in a complex messy partnership in Brazil. *Development in Practice*, *20*(8), 1027–1044.

Hafner-Burton, E. M., Kahler, M., & Montgomery, A. H. (2009). Network analysis for international relations. *International Organization*, *63*(3), 559. Retrieved from doi.org/10.1017/S0020818309090195

Hafner-Burton, E. M., & Montgomery, A. H. (2006). Power positions: International organizations, social networks, and conflict. *Journal of Conflict Resolution*, *50*(1), 3–27. Retrieved from doi.org/10.1177/0022002705281669

Hall, R., & Biersteker, T. (2002). The emergence of private authority in the international system. In R. Hall & T. Biersteker (Eds.), *The emergence of private authority in global governance* (pp. 3–22). Cambridge, UK: Cambridge University Press.

Hamid, M. (2016). The politics of language in education in a global polity. In K. Mundy, A. Green, R. Lingard, & A. Verger (Eds.), *Handbook of global policy and policy-making in education* (pp. 259–274). West Sussex, UK: Wiley-Blackwell.

Hogan, A., Sellar, S., & Lingard, B. (2016). Commercialising comparison: Pearson puts the TLC in soft capitalism. *Journal of Education Policy*, *31*(3), 243–258. Retrieved from doi.org/10.1080/02680939.2015.1112922

Howard, P. N. (2002). Network ethnography and the hypermedia organization: New media, new organizations, new methods. *New Media & Society*, *4*(4), 550–574. Retrieved from doi.org/10.1177/146144402321466813

Hughes, M., Peterson, L., Harrison, J., & Paxton, P. (2009). Power and relation in the world polity: The INGO network country score, 1978–1998. *Social Forces*, *87*(4), 1711–1742.

Hunjan, R., & Pettit, J. (2011). *Power: A practical guide for facilitating social change*. Dunfermline, UK: Carnegie UK Trust.

Independent Evaluation Group (IEG). (2011). *An independent assessment: The World Bank's involvement in global and regional partnership programs*. Washington, DC: World Bank.

Inter-Agency Network for Education in Emergencies (INEE). (2010). *Minimum standards for education: Preparedness, response, recovery*. Retrieved from https://inee.org/resources/inee-minimum-standards

Inter-Agency Network for Education in Emergencies (INEE). (2016). *Report from the INEE Global Consultation on Education Emergencies and Protracted Crises, Phase II*. Retrieved from https://archive.ineesite.org/en/eie-global-consultation-final-report

Inter-Agency Network for Education in Emergencies (INEE). (2018). *Who we are*. Retrieved from https://inee.org/us/who-we-are

International Education Funders Group (IEFG). (2018). *About us*. Retrieved from www.iefg.org/about

Jones, P. W. (2007). *World Bank financing of education: Lending, learning, and development* (2nd ed.). London, UK: Routledge.

Kahler, M. (Ed.). (2009). *Networked politics: Agency, power, and governance*. Itha-ca, NY: Cornell University Press.

Kaltmeier, O. (2015). Global South. In *Concepts of the Global South—Voices from around the world*. Cologne, Germany: Global South Studies Center.

Kamat, S. (2004). The privatization of public interest: Theorizing NGO discourse in a neoliberal era. *Review of International Political Economy, 11*(1), 155–176. Retrieved from doi.org/10.1080/0969229042000179794

Kaul, I., Conceicao. P., Le Goulven, K., & Mendoza, R. U. (2003). How to improve the provision of global public goods. In I. Kaul, P. Coceicao, K. LeGoulven, & R. U. Mendoza (Eds.), *Providing global public goods: Managing globalization* (pp. 21–58). New York, NY: United Nations Development Programme.

Keohane, R. (2006). Accountability in world politics. *Scandinavian Political Studies, 29*(2), 75–87.

Klees, S. J. (2008a). NGOs, civil society, and development: Is there a third way? *Current Issues in Comparative Education, 10*(1/2), 22–25.

Klees, S. J. (2008b). A quarter century of neoliberal thinking in education: Misleading analyses and failed policies. *Globalisation, Societies and Education, 6*(4), 311–348.

Klees, S. J. (2009). The language of education and development. In B. Brock-Utne & G. Garbo (Eds.), *Language and power: The implications of language for peace and development* (pp. 107–125). Dar es Salaam, Tanzania: Mkuki Na Nyota.

Klees, S. J., & Qargha, O. (2014). Equity in education: The case of UNICEF and the need for participative debate. *Prospects, 44*(3), 321–333. Retrieved from doi .org/10.1007/s11125-014-9295-0

Klees, S. J., Samoff, J., & Stromquist, N. P. (Eds.). (2012). *The World Bank and education*. Rotterdam, Netherlands: Sense. Retrieved from doi.org/10.1007/978 -94-6091-903-9

Lele, U., Sadik, N., & Simmons, A. (2007). *The changing aid architecture: Can global initiatives eradicate poverty?* Retrieved from https://www.global-philanthropy .org/pdf/aid_architecture_paper.pdf

Lister, S. (2000). *Power in partnership? An analysis of NGO's relationships with its partners*. CVO International Working Paper Number 5.

Magallanes, R. (2015). On the Global South. *Voices from Around the World: Concepts of the Global South, 2015*(1). Retrieved from voices.uni-koeln.de/2015-1

Magsino, S. (2009). *Applications of social network analysis for building community disaster resilience: Workshop summary*. Retrieved from www.nap.edu/read /12706/chapter/2

Mahler, A. (2018). Global South. In *Oxford bibliographies*. Retrieved from doi: 10.1093/OBO/9780190221911-0055

Martens, J. (2007). Multistakeholder partnerships—Future models of multilateralism? Retrieved from www.socialwatch.org/node/9571

McCowan, T., & Unterhalter, E. (2015). *Education and international development: An introduction*. London, UK: Bloomsbury Publishing.

McGoey, L. (2012). Philanthrocapitalism and its critics. *Poetics, 40*(2), 185–199. Retrieved from doi.org/10.1016/j.poetic.2012.02.006

McGrew, A. (2004). Power shift: From national government to global governance? In D. Held (Ed.), *A globalizing world? Culture, economics, politics* (2nd ed., pp. 127–167). London, UK: Routledge.

Menashy, F. (2009). Education as a global public good: The implications and applicability of a framework. *Globalisation, Societies, and Education, 7*(3), 307–320.

Menashy, F. (2013). Private-sector engagement in education worldwide: Conceptual and critical challenges. In A. Wiseman & E. Anderson (Eds.), *Annual review of comparative and international education* (pp. 137–165). Bingley, UK: Emerald Publishing.

Menashy, F. (2016). Understanding the roles of non-state actors in global governance: Evidence from the Global Partnership for Education. *Journal of Education Policy, 31*(1), 98–118. Retrieved from doi.org/10.1080/02680939.2015.1093176

Menashy, F. (2017). The limits of multi-stakeholder governance: The case of the Global Partnership for Education and private schooling. *Comparative Education Review, 61*(2), 240–268.

Menashy, F., & Dryden-Peterson, S. (2015). The Global Partnership for Education's evolving support to fragile and conflict-affected states. *International Journal of Educational Development, 44*(September), 82–94.

Menashy, F., & Read, R. (2016). Knowledge banking in global education policy: A bibliometric analysis of World Bank publications on public-private partnerships. *Education Policy Analysis Archives, 24*, 95. Retrieved from doi.org/10.14507/epaa.24.2523

Menashy, F., & Shields, R. (2017). Unequal partners? Networks, centrality, and aid to international education. *Comparative Education, 53*(4), 495–517. Retrieved from doi.org/10.1080/03050068.2017.1323822

Moaz, Z., Terris, L., Kuperman, R., & Talmud, I. (2003, February). *International relations: A network approach.* Paper presented at the Gilman Conference on New Directions in International Relations, New Haven, CT: Yale University.

Mokoro Limited. (2018) *Education Cannot Wait hosting review: Final report.* Oxford, UK: Author.

Morvaridi, B. (2012). Capitalist philanthropy and hegemonic partnerships. *Third World Quarterly, 33*(7), 1191–1210. Retrieved from doi.org/10.1080/01436597.2012.691827

Mundy, K. (2012). "Education for All" and the global governors. In D. Avant, M. Finnemore, & S. Sell (Eds.), *Who governs the globe?* (pp. 333–355). Cambridge, UK: Cambridge University Press.

Mundy, K., & Verger, A. (2015). The World Bank and the global governance of education in a changing world order. *International Journal of Educational Development, 40*, 9–18. Retrieved from doi.org/10.1016/j.ijedudev.2014.11.021

Muppidi, H. (2005). Colonial and postcolonial global governance. In M. Barnett & R. Duvall (Eds.), *Power in global governance* (pp. 273–293). Cambridge, UK: Cambridge University Press.

Naylor, T. (2011). Deconstructing development: The use of power and pity in the international development discourse. *International Studies Quarterly, 55*, 177–197.

Nye, J. (2004). *Soft power: The means to success in world politics.* New York, NY: Public Affairs.

OECD. (2016). Aid statistics by donor, recipient and sector. https://www.oecd.org/dac/stats/aid-at-a-glance.htm

Organisation for Economic Co-operation and Development (OECD). (1996). *Shaping the 21st century: The contribution of development co-operation*. Paris: Author. Retrieved from www.oecd.org/dac/2508761.pdf

Organisation for Economic Co-operation and Development (OECD). (2005). *The Paris declaration on aid effectiveness and the Accra Agenda for Action*. Retrieved from www.oecd.org/dac/effectiveness/34428351.pdf

Organisation for Economic Co-operation and Development (OECD). (2008). *The Accra Agenda for Action*. Retrieved from https://www.oecd.org/dac/effectiveness/45827311.pdf

Organisation for Economic Co-operation and Development (OECD). (2011). *Busan Partnership for Effective Development Cooperation Fourth High-Level Forum on Aid*. Retrieved from www.oecd.org/development/effectiveness/busanpartnership.htm

Organisation for Economic Co-operation and Development (OECD). (2012). *Aid effectiveness 2011: Progress in implementing the Paris Declaration*. Retrieved from www.oecd.org/dac/aid-effectiveness-2011-9789264125780-en.htm

Organisation for Economic Co-operation and Development (OECD). (2015). *Development co-operation report 2015: Making partnerships effective coalitions for action*. Paris: Author. dx.doi.org/10.1787/dcr-2015-en

Overseas Development Institute (ODI). (2016). *Education cannot wait: Proposing a fund for education in emergencies*. London, UK: Author.

Oxfam. (2016). *Understanding networks: The application of social network analysis methodology in the South Caucasus context*. Retrieved from policy-practice.oxfam.org.uk/publications/understanding-networks-the-application-of-social-network-analysis-methodology-i-620117

Pennycook, A. (2000). *English and the discourses of colonialism*. London, UK: Routledge.

Phillipson, R. (1997). Realities and myths of linguistic imperialism. *Journal of Multilingual and Multicultural Development, 18*(3), 238–248.

Picciotto, R. (2002). *Development cooperation and performance evaluation: The Monterrey challenge*. Washington, DC: World Bank.

Pretty, J. (1995). Participatory learning for sustainable agriculture, *World Development, 23*(8), 1247–1263.

Ramalingam, B. (2013). *Aid on the edge of chaos: Rethinking international cooperation in a complex world*. Oxford, UK: Oxford University Press.

Ravelo, J. L., & Jones, R. (2014, June 27). *What the private sector wants from the GPE*. Retrieved from www.devex.com/news/what-the-private-sector-wants-from-the-gpe-83778

Read, R. (2019). Knowledge counts: Influential actors in the Education for All Global Monitoring Report knowledge network. *International Journal of Educational Development, 64*, 96–105.

Reckhow, S. (2013). *Follow the money: How foundation dollars change public school politics*. Oxford, UK: Oxford University Press.

Reinicke, W. (1999). The other world wide web: Global public policy networks. *Foreign Policy, 117*, 44–57.

Rhodes, R. (2007). Understanding governance: Ten years on. *Organization Studies, 28*, 1243–1264.

Riddell, R. (2007). *Does foreign aid really work?* Oxford, UK: Oxford University Press.

Riddell, R. (2014). *Does foreign aid really work? An updated assessment* (Development Policy Centre discussion paper 33). Canberra: Crawford School of Public Policy, Australian National University.

Rizvi, F., & Lingard, B. (2010). *Globalizing education policy.* New York, NY: Routledge.

Robertson, S., Mundy, K., Verger, A., & Menashy, F. (Eds.). (2012). *Public private partnerships in education: New actors and modes of governance in a globalizing world.* Cheltenham, UK: Edward Elgar.

Rose, P., & Steer, L. (2013). *Financing for global education: Opportunities for multilateral action.* Washington, DC: Brookings.

Ruggie, J. G. (2004). Reconstituting the global public domain—Issues, actors, and practices. *European Journal of International Relations, 10*(4), 499–531.

Rupert, M. (2005). Class powers and the politics of global governance. In M. Barnett & R. Duvall (Eds.), *Power in global governance* (pp. 205–228). Cambridge, UK: Cambridge University Press.

Sachs, J. (2015). *Financing education for all.* Retrieved from www.project-syndicate .org/commentary/financing-education-poor-children-by-jeffrey-d-sachs-2015-03

Samoff, J., & Carrol, B. (2004). The promise of partnership and continuities of dependence: External support to higher education in Africa. *African Studies Review, 47*(1), 67.

Savedoff, W. D. (2012). *Global government, mixed coalitions, and the future of international cooperation.* Washington, DC: Center for Global Development.

Schiffer, E., & Waale, D. (2008). *Tracing power and influence in networks: Net-Map as a tool for research and strategic network planning* (IFPRI discussion papers No. 772). Washington, DC: International Food Policy Research Institute (IFPRI). Retrieved from ideas.repec.org/p/fpr/ifprid/772.html

Scholte, J. A., (2002). Civil society and democracy in global governance. *Global Governance, 8*(3), 281–304.

Scholte, J. A., & Söderbaum, F. (2017). A changing global development agenda? *Forum for Development Studies, 44*(1), 1–12.

Severino, J. M., & Ray, O. (2010). *The end of ODA (II): The birth of hypercollective action* (Working Paper No. 218). Washington, DC: Center for Global Development. Retrieved from doi.org/10.2139/ssrn.1646605

Shafik, M. (2009, June 19). *From architecture to networks: Aid in a world of variable geometry.* Retrieved from ideas4development.org/en/from-architecture-to -networks-aid-in-a-world-of-variable-geometry

Srivastava, P. (2016). Questioning the global scaling-up of low-fee private schooling: The nexus between business, philanthropy, and PPPs. In A. Verger, C. Lubienski, & G. Steiner-Khamsi (Eds.), *The global education industry—World yearbook of education 2016* (pp. 248–263). New York, NY: Routledge.

Srivastava, P., & Oh, S. A. (2010). Private foundations, philanthropy, and partnership in education and development: Mapping the terrain. *International Journal of Educational Development, 30*(5), 460–471.

Steiner-Khamsi, G., & Draxler, A. (2018). *The state, business, and education: Public–private partnerships revisited.* Cheltenham, UK: Edward Elgar.

Stenson, B. (2010). *Strengths and weaknesses in the governance of selected global health initiatives.* Retrieved from www.globalpartnership.org/content/strengths-and-weaknesses-governance-selected-global-health-initiatives-report

Stone, D. (2008). Global public policy, transnational policy communities, and their networks. *Policy Studies Journal, 36*(1), 19–38.

Tansey, O. (2007). Process tracing and elite interviewing: A case for non-probability sampling. *PS: Political Science & Politics, 40*(4), 765–772.

Tataryn, M., & Blanchet, K. (2012). *Evaluation of post-earthquake physical rehabilitation response in Haiti—A systems analysis.* Retrieved from blogs.lshtm.ac.uk/disabilitycentre/files/2012/04/Haiti-giving-with-one-hand.pdf

TheirWorld. (2018, April 19). *How partnerships can help to tackle the global education crisis.* Retrieved from theirworld.org/news/live-blog-global-business-coalition-for-education-partnerships-can-tackle-learning-crisis

Torfason, M., & Ingram, P. (2010). The global rise of democracy: A network account. *American Sociological Review, 75*(3), 355–377.

UNESCO. (2000). *Education for All and the Dakar Framework for Action.* Retrieved from unesdoc.unesco.org/ark:/48223/pf0000121147

United Nations (UN). (2003). *Financing for development: Monterrey consensus of the International Conference on Financing for Development.* Retrieved from https://www.un.org/en/development/desa/population/migration/generalassembly/docs/globalcompact/A_CONF.198_11.pdf

United Nations (UN). (2013). *UN system task team on the post-2015 UN Development Agenda: A renewed global partnership for development.* Retrieved from www.un.org/en/development/desa/policy/untaskteam_undf/them_tp2.shtml

United Nations (UN). (2015a. August). Ban hails UN member states' agreement on "people's agenda" to end poverty, promote sustainability. *UN News.* Retrieved from news.un.org/en/story/2015/08/505552-ban-hails-un-member-states-agreement-peoples-agenda-end-poverty-promote#.Vb83MmOp2Sp

United Nations (UN). (2015b). *Statement by the secretary-general following agreement on the outcome document of the post-2015 development agenda.* Retrieved from www.un.org/sg/en/content/sg/statement/2015-08-02/statement-secretary-general-following-agreement-outcome-document

United Nations (UN). (2015c). *Transforming our world: The 2030 Agenda for Sustainable Development.* Retrieved from sustainabledevelopment.un.org/post2015/transformingourworld

United Nations (UN). (2016). *Sustainable development knowledge platform: Multi-stakeholder partnerships.* Retrieved from sustainabledevelopment.un.org/sdinaction

United Nations Development Programme (UNDP). (2018) *SDG Goal 17: Partnership for the goals.* Retrieved from www.undp.org/content/undp/en/home/sustainable-development-goals/goal-17-partnerships-for-the-goals.html

United Nations Girls' Education Initiative (UNGEI). (2018). *About us.* Retrieved from www.ungei.org/whatisungei

United Nations Office for the Coordination of Humanitarian Affairs (OCHA) (2017). *Community engagement at the centre of disaster response.* Retrieved from www.unocha.org/story/community-engagement-centre-disaster-response

Utting, P., & Zammit, A. (2009). United Nations-business partnerships: Good intentions and contradictory agendas. *Journal of Business Ethics, 90*, 39–56.

van Fleet, J. (2011). *A global education challenge: Harnessing corporate philanthropy to educate the world's poor.* Washington, DC: Brookings Institution.

van Fleet, J. (2012). *Scaling up corporate social investments in education: Five strategies that work.* Washington, DC: Brookings Institution.

Vavrus, F., & Bartlett, L. (Eds.). (2009). *Critical approaches to comparative education: Vertical case studies from Africa, Europe, the Middle East, and the Americas.* London, UK: Palgrave MacMillan.

Vavrus, F., & Seghers, M. (2010). Critical discourse analysis in comparative education: A discursive study of "partnership" in Tanzania's poverty reduction policies. *Comparative Education Review, 54*(1), 77–103. Retrieved from doi.org /10.1086/647972

Vennesson, P. (2008). Case studies and process tracing: Theories and practices. In D. Della Porta & M. Keating (Eds.), *Approaches and methodologies in the social sciences* (pp. 223–239). New York, NY: Cambridge University Press.

Verger, A. (2012). Framing and selling global education policy: The promotion of public–private partnerships for education in low-income contexts. *Journal of Education Policy, 27*(1), 109–130. Retrieved from doi.org/10.1080/02680939 .2011.623242

Verger, A., Fontdevila, C., & Zancajo, A. (2016). *The privatization of education: A political economy of global education reform.* New York, NY: Teachers College Press.

Wallerstein, I. (2004). *World-systems analysis: An introduction.* Durham, NC: Duke University Press.

Wasserman, S., & Faust, K. (1994). *Social network analysis: Methods and applications.* Cambridge, UK: Cambridge University Press.

Watkins, K. (2016). *No lost generation: Holding to the promise of education for all Syrian refugees.* Retrieved from theirworld.org/resources/detail/no-lost-generation-holding-to-the-promise-of-education-for-all-syrian-refugees

White, S. C. (1996). Depoliticising development: The uses and abuses of participation, *Development in Practice, 6*(1), 6–15.

Wolfensohn, J. D. (1998). *The other crisis.* Retrieved from www.imf.org/external/am /1998/speeches/pr03e.pdf

World Bank. (2005). *Fast Track Initiative: Building a global compact for education.* Retrieved from siteresources.worldbank.org/EDUCATION/Resources/Education -Notes/EdNotes_FastTrack.pdf

World Bank. (2014). *The Global Partnership for Education and the World Bank Group: The facts.* Retrieved from www.worldbank.org/en/topic/education /brief/the-global-partnership-for-education-and-the-world-bank-group-the -facts

World Bank (2018a). *The International Finance Facility for Education: Joint statement by multilateral development banks.* Retrieved from www.worldbank.org /en/news/statement/2018/05/11/the-international-finance-facility-for-education -joint-statement-by-multilateral-development-banks

World Bank (2018b, July 26). *New inclusive education initiative for children with disabilities announced by DFID, Norad, and the World Bank.* Retrieved from www.worldbank.org/en/news/press-release/2018/07/26/new-inclusive-education -initiative-for-children-with-disabilities-announced-by-dfid-norad-and-the-world -bank

World Humanitarian Summit (WHS). (2014). *Regional consultation, North and South-East Asia*. Retrieved from www.agendaforhumanity.org/sites/default/files/resources/2017/Jul/WHS_Regional_Consultation_NSEA_Final_Report_LIGHT.pdf

World Humanitarian Summit (WHS). (2016). *Connecting business: Special session*. Retrieved from whsturkey.org/Contents/Upload/SS%2012%20Connecting%20Businesses_isuem45t.rjt.pdf

Index

About the Author

Francine Menashy is an associate professor in the Department of Leadership in Education at the University of Massachusetts Boston. Her research explores global education policy, international aid to education and private-sector engagement, focusing on transnational partnerships and support in contexts of humanitarian crisis. She has served as an advisor to several global civil society organizations, UN agencies, and international financial institutions. She holds a PhD from the University of Toronto and is coeditor of *Comparative Education Review.*